Systematic
Instruction

Companion Audiovisual Materials

A set of filmstrip-tape instructional programs coordinated with the contents of this book is available from Vimcet Associates Inc., P.O. Box 24714, Los Angeles, California, 90024. Information regarding these materials is available upon request.

Systematic Instruction

W. James Popham

Eva L. Baker

Graduate School of Education

University of California, Los Angeles

PRENTICE-HALL, INC.
Englewood Cliffs, New Jersey

Prentice-Hall International, Inc., *London*
Prentice-Hall of Australia, Pty. Ltd., *Sydney*
Prentice-Hall of Canada, Ltd., *Toronto*
Prentice-Hall of India Private Limited, *New Delhi*
Prentice-Hall of Japan, Inc., *Tokyo*

Preface

This book is designed for those who wish to learn about the nature of instruction. For those preparing to be teachers, the text will serve as an introduction to the kinds of considerations associated with the teaching act. For already experienced teachers, the text will provide a vehicle for re-examining general instructional strategies and particular teaching tactics.

The need for this kind of a book arose from the authors' experience in working with pre-service and in-service public school teachers. For a number of years now, we have been advocating a systematic approach to instructional decision-making. We have attempted to persuade teachers that it is possible to bring intellectual rigor to an arena where the use of folklore and a "bag of tricks" has been customary.

Frankly, we were loath to embark on this writing effort. It would have been far easier to select from the shelf an already published textbook which presented, at least in general, the kind of position we endorsed. Unfortunately, there simply weren't any such books. The bulk of texts dealing with methods of instruction seemed to us, in spite of a number of salutory features, considerably off the mark with respect to promoting systematic approaches to instruction. Times are changing in education, and hard thinking regarding instructional matters is more and more common. We hope that this text is consonant with that trend.

The text can be used by those preparing for teaching at all levels, kindergarten through college. It is hoped that a number of practicing teachers will give some attention to the positions advocated in the following pages. Although it can be used separately, it was designed to be employed in conjunction with two other texts, each consisting of a set of self-instructional programs. The material treated in those programs is, in some cases, an elaboration of topics examined in this book. The sets of programs referred to are *Establishing Instructional Goals* and *Planning an Instructional Sequence*, both of which are published by Prentice-Hall, Inc.

W.J.P.
E.L.B.

Los Angeles, California

Contents

8.   Classroom Management   117

9.   The Evaluation of Instruction   129

10.   The Teacher as an Experimenter   149

Index   161

1

Intuition Versus Verification

The Teacher

In all societies, from least to most civilized, the teacher plays a critical role. The teacher, with few exceptions, is one of the chief molders of the future members of a society. True, some societies recognize the teacher's importance in more tangible ways than others; but even in this country, where teacher salaries often are lower than one might prefer, there is no doubt that the teacher's responsibility is profound. Many parents, as they send their youngster off to school each day, occasionally experience qualms regarding the ability of their child's teacher. And most teachers, after a few months on their first teaching assignment, are already aware of the great potential influence they may have in shaping their pupils' minds. Yet, this widespread awareness of the magnitude of the teacher's responsibility tragically has not been translated into teachers' efforts to make careful instructional decisions.

It is not surprising that many teachers are relatively unsophisticated regarding the instructional process. The majority have been trained through the use of approaches that border on

1

the mystical. Most teacher-preparation sequences in American institutions foster a form of imitative behavior in prospective teachers. In the handful of required courses prior to student teaching, the teacher-candidate is usually offered a series of abstruse principles ("Intermittent reinforcement of a response promotes greater resistance to extinction.") or a number of "common sense" and occasionally obtuse suggestions for classroom practice ("Be consistent.") or both. Then the hardly prepared candidate is tossed into student teaching, where he presumably learns about the instructional process from an experienced supervising teacher.

Unfortunately, despite observers' enthusiastic endorsements, student-teaching experiences usually do not help the prospective teacher learn how to teach. Rather, the candidate learns how to "get through the day." He loves the experience because he feels he is mastering some of the required teaching skills. But what the student teacher often masters is only the ability to parrot the supervising teacher. Since the standards by which a student teacher is to be judged are typically elusive, the wise student teacher often chooses to emulate the style and general approach of the supervising teacher. After all, it is usually the supervising teacher who determines the all-important (for job placement) student-teaching grade. What right-minded supervising teacher could fail to give a high grade to a carbon copy of himself? Thus, with no more rigorous criteria to guide them, both student teacher and supervising teacher fall into a game of mimicry. The fewer the times the student teacher deviates from the image of his master, the better the grade he earns.

This unthinking duplication is, of course, not found everywhere. But there are too many instances in which the first-year teacher enters the classroom with nothing more than a collection of borrowed procedures.

Even during the teacher's early years on the job after the completion of teacher-education experiences, the situation is not

Note — supervisor of student tchr model') teaching that the
supervisor has well control.

much improved. A beginning teacher is often judged by administrators and supervisors who use largely ambiguous criteria in evaluating instruction. A supervisor faults a teacher who doesn't "do it the way I did when I was in the classroom." Unclear standards for judging instructional competency lead to a confusion on the part of all concerned regarding what good teaching is and how it should be promoted. It is small wonder that the bulk of American teachers view the instructional process as a simplistic enterprise, intuitively derived and not subject to careful scrutiny.

For generations we have been transmitting teaching skills by a process much like the "laying on of hands." Some sensitive teachers improve their skills as they gather years of experience; but others unfortunately repeat the first year's experience many times. They simply don't profit from it.

Happily, the situation is changing. We are becoming increasingly conversant with the intricacies of instruction. It is now possible to transmit to teachers a set of tangible competencies that will aid them in their instructional endeavors. Just a few decades ago this could not have been said with much conviction; but now we do have some sound principles (although they are far from polished) to guide the teacher interested in improving his instruction.

The Inspired and the Professional

Not every teacher needs help. There is some truth in the assertion that "Teachers are born, not made." Some teachers *are* born—they are the individuals who never really think carefully about the way they teach, yet by almost any standards they are superlative instructors. Such people don't need much, if any, help in improving their teaching. They are, indeed, almost *inspired* teachers; certainly they are inspirational.

There are also individuals who will never be skilled instructors, no matter how much systematic attention they devote to improving themselves. They may have personality or intellectual attributes that are antithetical to high-level instruction. For a few people, no amount of remediation will help them teach better. There are some human attributes that are very difficult to modify. It is next to impossible to make a human being much "smarter," even though we might like to do so. It is also very difficult to make a thoroughgoing introvert an extrovert, or to make a poor public speaker a skilled orator.

But for the vast majority of individuals who are interested in being effective teachers, there are currently methods of approaching that task that will markedly increase instructional skill. There is a way of viewing instruction so that one can improve the quality of the *intellectual decisions* the teacher makes about his teaching activities. The approach advocated in this text is based on one such conception of instruction, namely, an instructional model that permits the teacher (1) to select instructional activities likely to be successful and (2) to evaluate the adequacy of those decisions so that he may, over time, improve the quality of his instruction. Teachers who approach the task of improving themselves through the use of such systematic schemes should be considered real professionals. They are thoroughly competent practitioners who can use the special knowledge of their field to improve themselves. They may not be as inspired as the "born" teacher, but in the end they can be every bit as inspirational—to their colleagues as well as to their students.

The Need for a Simple
Instructional Model

Teaching is extremely complex. No one who has dealt with thirty diverse youngsters in an elementary or secondary school classroom can quarrel with this assertion. One can study the subtle and varied interactions among teacher, pupils, subject matter, classroom, and cultural environment, study them to the point where the complexities are overwhelming. Even though instructional operations are so fantastically complicated, it is still possible to make substantial improvements in them through the use of very simple instructional models. The unfortunate truth is that teachers aren't using very efficiently the insights that we have right now. If one studies classroom convolutions until most of the interactions affecting instruction are thoroughly understood, years of study will accumulate—and there will be generations of children who will fail to benefit from the modest yet powerful instructional advances with which we are now conversant.

The approach in this text, therefore, is to present and advocate a very simple instructional model, rather than one that attempts to take account of the total complexity of the teaching act. We wish you to become thoroughly familiar with this modest instructional model so that, in putting it into use, you will derive the clear advantages available from it. Too many texts dealing with instruction "cover the waterfront," identifying every possible principle relevant to instruction. After finishing the book, the reader is often thoroughly confused. It is difficult to weld together a workable approach to instruction when one has so many alternatives from which to choose. The instructional model offered here can be readily mastered, yet is powerful enough to make a real difference in what youngsters learn.

The primary purpose of this book, then, is to present a system that you can use to improve what you do in the classroom. The model described herein is perfectly adaptable to different personality types. Teaching is always a very personal act. It should be personal; it should also be effective; and it can be fun. An examination of an efficient instructional model, and its implications for the intellectual decisions that all teachers must make, will constitute the remainder of this text.

2

A Goal-Referenced Instructional Model

There are many ways of thinking about instruction. A beginning teacher, faced with the necessity of deciding what will take place during his first session in the classroom, usually asks the following question: "What shall I do?" This is a very realistic question, for in most personal decisions people try to consider what they have to do. Yet, in the case of instruction, it is the wrong question. The proper question that any teacher should ask himself is: "What do I want my learners to become?"

The danger with asking the question "What shall I do?" is that it focuses the teacher's attention on the wrong things. As he considers the activities he might carry out in the classroom, the neophyte teacher frequently thinks back over his own experiences as a pupil. He may recall particularly good instructors that he had in elementary school, secondary school, or college, and he often tries to emulate some of the procedures they employed. He may think of other classroom events such as class discussions, guest speakers, panel reports, the use of motion-picture films, and audio tapes. He may even consider the use of more divergent activities such as field trips, sociodramas, or nondirective teaching. In all of these considerations,

7

he will be focusing on alternative procedures that he might employ in the classroom. Note that attention is given primarily to the *instructional means* that he will use rather than to the results that these means are supposed to produce.

In the case of the beginning teacher, it is possible that his selection will be guided by one overriding motive—to fill time. Most beginning teachers fear the prospect of ending a class period twenty minutes early and then having nothing planned to do more than anything else. They will select almost any instructional activity that promises to "look instructional" and occupy time. During his second year of instruction, after an initial year of such time-filling activities, the teacher has good reason for continuing the same activities—he has already used them once. He may forget that the activities, initially selected on the most expedient grounds, have no other reason for existence than that they have been used once before.

Teaching Effectiveness

Although the search has been less fervent than the quest for the Holy Grail, there is a long history of educators who have sought a clear definition of teaching competence. For years educational researchers and theorists have attempted to reach a satisfactory conception of "the effective teacher." Generally, approaches to this task have been too simplistic. There has been an attempt to identify *the* good teacher in terms of definite attributes he possessed or certain classroom procedures he employed. More recently it has been recognized that there is no generic entity such as "the effective teacher." Rather, teaching effectiveness must be considered in relationship to a *particular* instructor, dealing with *particular* learners, in a *particular* environment, as he attempts to achieve *particular* instructional goals.

Even though educators have departed, to some extent, from former inadequate conceptions of "overall" teacher compe-

tence, there is a lingering corollary of that conception that
needs to be discarded—namely, that teaching efficiency should
be judged in terms of the instructional means the teacher
employs.

Means-Referenced Instructional Models

Many educators believe that by watching a teacher in a classroom the observer can draw satisfactory inferences regarding
the teacher's instructional competence. This is the assumption
on which most public school supervisory schemes are based.
A supervisor visits the teacher's classroom and notes the procedures used by that teacher, such as the manner in which
questions are addressed to pupils, the teacher's handling of
pupil responses, or his chalkboard procedures. The supervisor
then meets with the teacher to discuss ways of "improving his
techniques." These discussions are based on the assumption
that the supervisor knows something about which techniques
are preferable. Very often, the only standards that a supervisor
has in judging someone's else's teaching procedures are based
on the procedures he himself used when he was an instructor.
An uncountable number of classroom teachers are given ad-
verse evaluations simply because they happen to behave at
variance with the supervisor's recollection of his own stellar
days in the classroom.

Many educational researchers are also attempting to deal with
the question of instructional competence largely in terms of
the classroom procedures used by teachers. In recent years
extromoly complicated procedures have been developed for
observing what goes on in the classroom. Observers are asked
to rate every few seconds of "teacher talk" or "pupil talk,"
the number of "positive" or "negative" responses made by
learners, and so on. Indeed, we can safely predict that in several years observation devices will be available whereby every

few milliseconds an observer will be obliged to record several dozen observational judgments.

The problem with all of these attempts to define the good teacher is that they are based on an inadequate conception of instructional effectiveness. They rarely, if ever, raise the more important question of *what happens to the learners* as a consequence of the procedures used in the classroom—and this, after all, is the critical question. The only reason for a teacher's existence in the classroom is to modify the behavior of his learners. Effective instruction, therefore, should be defined as an ability to bring about desirable modifications in the abilities and perceptions of the learner. If an instructor uses particularly esteemed procedures but fails to accomplish measurable change in his learners, how can we possibly judge that instructor to be effective? There is considerable research evidence indicating that no single teacher action is invariably associated with learner achievement. This is, of course, a very reasonable finding. As we indicated earlier, the nature of instruction is so particularized that the procedures that may work magnificently for one teacher may fail for another teacher. Some teachers, for example, might be very adept discussion leaders, yet for certain learners and certain instructional objectives, discussion approaches may be inappropriate. Other teachers who might be able to use authoritarian methods of instruction very skillfully find situations in which such methods produce unsatisfactory responses in learners. The personal characteristics that blend together to form a teacher are obviously so variable that what works for one teacher cannot necessarily be expected to work for a colleague.

In summary, conceptions of instruction that are means-referenced are inadequate for purposes of a teacher's instructional decision-making. Instead of asking the question "What shall I do?" the teacher must ask a different kind of question—a question based on a goal-referenced instructional model.

Goal-Referenced Instructional Models

For several years there has been an encouraging emphasis in this country on the desirability of a teacher's thinking clearly about his instructional goals. We shall describe the merits of this movement in more detail in the next chapter; here it is sufficient to point out that the most important advantage of the emphasis on specificity in instructional objectives is that it forces the teacher to think about the right question: "What do I want my learners to become?" A goal-referenced instructional model attends initially to the question of what observable behaviors the learner should possess at the conclusion of instruction. After the desired learner behaviors, that is, the goals, are clearly specified, the selection of instructional means becomes must simpler and, in general, far more effective. For example, if a teacher has an extremely clear conception of the kinds of competencies that the learners are to display at the conclusion of a three-week instructional sequence, he can build into the instructional unit opportunities for the learners to practice behaviors consistent with those desired objectives He does not have to select activities merely to fill time, but if time-filling does become a consideration, at least he can provide practice relevant to the desired terminal behaviors. This selection of relevant practice activities, or activities that may be necessary precursors to that practice, is far easier in a situation where specific objectives are known in advance.

A principal advantage, therefore, of a goal-referenced instructional model is that it *aids the teacher in the initial selection of instructional activities*. Activities can be selected, both for the teacher and for the learners, that are more likely to promote the learners' attainment of instructional goals.

A second and perhaps even more important advantage of a

goal-referenced instructional model is that it *permits the teacher, over time, to improve the quality of an instructional sequence*. What does a teacher do when he employs a means-referenced instructional model to improve his instruction? At the conclusion of an instructional sequence, such as a four-week unit, how does he know whether the instructional procedures he has been using should be maintained or modified? Unfortunately, such a teacher doesn't have any definite standards to guide his decision. He is likely to make mistakes. He may decide to maintain an instructional procedure that is not producing desirable results with learners, or he may decide to discard an effective instructional sequence. His problem is that he has no clear standard against which to judge the efficacy of his instructional procedures.

A teacher using a goal-referenced instructional model, however, has very clear standards on which to base decisions regarding modification of instructional procedures. He observes the post-instruction behavior of learners. Can the learners, at the end of instruction, demonstrate the behaviors originally described in the instructional objectives? In other words, have the goals been achieved? If they have, the instructor is relatively satisfied and will usually not revise his instructional procedures. If they haven't been achieved, he must make changes in the instructional sequence.

The value of having clear standards by which to judge whether to make changes in instruction cannot be overemphasized. Most teachers behave with a kind of intuitive abandon at the end of instruction. They may respond to an *atypical* student's comments such as, "That was an interesting unit," or "That was sure a dull class!" Such responses may lead the teacher to make the wrong decisions regarding instruction. Further, teachers are notoriously poor judges of learner responses. Many times, for example, teachers will consider a class session successful because it was entertaining; if the criterion for success had been *learning* rather than entertainment, a more negative judgment would have had to be made.

Instructors can be easily deceived by the "nodder." The nodder is a student who seems to have the ability to nod at just the right times. As the instructor makes a key point, the nodder will invariably indicate his concurrence by a sharp up-and-down motion of the head. After a few weeks of these incisive nods, the instructor is assured that the nodder is moving with him intellectually through the substance of the course. He knows that the nodder is thinking with him and looks forward with anticipation to that student's outstanding performance on the unit examination. It has been our unfortunate experience that the nodder usually fails our exams. This is testimony to the fact that teachers often can't judge very well whether their class is proceeding satisfactorily unless they have some guidelines by which to make that judgment. Such guidance is provided by the use of a goal-referenced instructional model.

The Instructional Model

The instructional model advocated in this text is a scheme featuring four essentially distinct operations. The model emphasizes the intellectual decision-making the teacher engages in *prior* to and *after* instruction and, as such, is really more of a planning and assessment model than a "teaching procedures" scheme. *First*, the objectives of instruction are specified in terms of learner behavior. *Second*, the student is preassessed as to his current status with respect to those instructional objectives. *Third*, instructional activities that should bring about the intended objectives are designed. And *fourth*, the student's attainment of the objectives is evaluated. The major

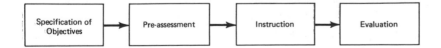

Figure 1. *A Goal-Referenced
Instructional Model*

components of this instructional scheme are depicted diagrammatically in Figure 1. Although all four of these components will be treated in more extensive detail throughout the remainder of the volume, a brief description of each is given here.

Specification of Objectives

The instructional objectives in this four-component model must be specified in terms of learner post-instruction behavior. Almost every educator concedes the importance of objectives, but until recently few have advocated that they be described in explicit terms of how the learner is supposed to behave at the conclusion of instruction. The present instructional scheme requires that goals be stated in unambiguous terms of learner behavior.

Pre-assessment

The second step in this instructional model requires the teacher to identify the learner's entry behavior. The term "pre-assessment" is used rather than "pretesting" only because pre-assessment may suggest more varied assessment procedures than the use of paper and pencil tests. One of the real advantages of pre-assessment is in discovering whether the student *already* has in his repertoire the kind of behavior the teacher wishes to promote. It is conceivable that students may enter a course with far more competence than the teacher anticipates, and that literally weeks may be wasted while students are "taught" that which they already know. In the same vein, it is often the case that students know far *less* than the teacher assumes. They may actually fail to possess the ability, knowledge, and skills that they need in order to accomplish the intended instructional objectives. In either case, the results of pre-assessment may suggest modifications that should be made in the originally selected objectives. For instance, an analysis of the student's entry behavior may result in a decision to add or delete certain goals.

A particularly important advantage of pre-assessment is that it can establish with a high degree of accuracy that the student cannot, in advance of instruction, perform well with respect to the intended objectives. When, after instruction, the learner is able to behave in the prescribed fashion, the teacher's instructional efforts will deserve credit for achieving those behavior changes.

An additional advantage of pre-assessment is that through its use the teacher can identify individuals within the class for whom he may wish to vary either the instructional objectives or the instructional procedures.

Instruction

Once he has pre-assessed the learner, and possibly modified the instructional objectives, the teacher next designs an instructional sequence that he hopes will accomplish the intended objectives. This operation is very complicated; but after the precise explication of the intended objectives, it is far less difficult. As later chapters will indicate, principles drawn from instructional psychology can be of great utility in aiding the teacher to design instructional sequences. For example, there is a principle known as *appropriate practice*, which demands that the teacher provide opportunities for the learner to practice the behavior called for in the instructional objective. This means that if the teacher intends to have the learners acquire a particular skill, he must give them an opportunity to practice that skill during the instructional sequence. As a consequence, one of the first things that a teacher must do if he adheres to this principle is build in appropriate practice opportunities during the instructional sequence.

As the teacher designs an instructional sequence, the more sophistication he has regarding the selection of instructional means, the more probable will be the attainment of desirable results. In subsequent chapters we shall describe several principles that will enable the teacher to (1) analyze the tasks the learner must master and (2) provide instructional situations that should accomplish the learning of those tasks.

Evaluation

The fourth step in the instructional model is to evaluate the degree to which learners have achieved the instructional goals. It is at this juncture that the instructor determines whether the students can actually behave as he planned when he formulated his objectives. The development of a specific evaluation procedure, such as the preparation of a test, was undoubtedly largely resolved when the objectives were originally specified. In some instances very specific instructional objectives include statements of the evaluation procedures. Objectives and evaluation should, in essence, be identical; that is, test items should be drawn from the class of behavior specified in the objectives. The point is that the evaluation here is not of the learner, but of the adequacy of the decisions reached by the instructor. We are not trying to determine whether Johnny gets an "A" or a "B," but whether the instructional plans made by the teacher were adequate and whether his implementation of those plans was adequate. In the instructional model we advocate in this volume, unachieved objectives are generally viewed as reflecting inadequacies in instruction. This means that when learners fail to attain the prespecified goals, something was wrong with the teacher, either with the plans he made or with the way he carried them out.

On the other hand, if the instructional objectives *are* achieved, the teacher deserves all the credit. He ought to consider the possibility of augmenting his objectives so that he achieves even more, but he should obviously be pleased when his goals are achieved—particularly if he has demonstrated through pre-assessment that, prior to instruction, the learner could not behave in the intended manner.

In Figure 2 we consider common courses of action suggested by pupil post-instruction performance. The self-correction features of the instructional model should be apparent. Modifications are made in the instructional sequence or objectives

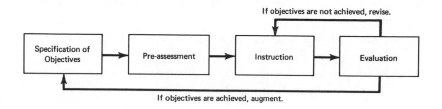

Figure 2. *Courses of Action Dictated by Evaluation of Results*

only as a result of learner data. The instructional sequence is improved and the objectives are made more challenging.

Focus: The Learner

In general, the instructional model that we are advocating requires that the teacher be attentive to the learner. The focus is on the student, not the teacher. This focus is clearly indicated by the inadequacy of the question "What shall I, the teacher, do?" For too many years educators have been concerned with what happens to the teacher, not with what happens to the learner. The time for that misdirected concern is over. The sensible conception of instruction is a goal-referenced model. We must set out systematically to improve the degree to which teachers can attain prespecified objectives with learners. The teacher who becomes more skilled in this task becomes more professionally competent. The competent teacher, therefore, is the one who can more efficiently use a goal-referenced instructional model such as the one described in the following pages.

ADDITIONAL READING

De Cecco, John P. (ed.), *Educational Technology: Readings in Programmed Instruction* (New York: Holt, Rinehart & Winston, Inc., 1964).

Mager, Robert F., *Developing Attitudes Toward Learning* (Palo Alto, Calif.: Fearon Publishers, Inc., 1968).

Tyler, Ralph, *Basic Principles of Curriculum and Instruction* (Chicago: The University of Chicago Press, 1950).

3
Instructional Objectives

For years teachers have been told by those in authority to develop instructional objectives. Perhaps it was a professor during teacher education days who said something classic like, "You can't tell where you're going without a road map." Maybe it was a school principal who demanded a set of course objectives before the first class meeting of the academic year. Or it may have been a supervisor who began a post-observation session by a question such as, "What were your goals for today?" In spite of the lip service that objectives have received over the past several hundred years, few teachers have derived many instructional dividends from expressing their goals because, ordinarily, the objectives have been stated in terms too loose to allow the teacher to proceed effectively from them.

Since the early 1960's, however, a development of major significance has been underway regarding the statement of instructional goals. Perhaps because of the pioneering work in programed instruction or because of a general turn toward technology in our country, whatever the reason, educators have been urged since that time to describe their objectives, not in the customary vague manner, but *in terms of measurable learner behavior.* In our view this development is one of the most important educational advances of the 1900's and signals a very significant attack upon the problems of education. Precise objectives are the basis of the four-component instructional model advocated in this text.

Operationally Stated
Objectives

What is the difference between the kinds of objectives that educators are now being urged to state and the kinds that they have been told to develop in the past? In former times teachers were told to write objectives in terms of what was to be covered in the course. Such objectives would describe the topics or concepts that they would treat during the class—for example, "The course will cover the important events leading up to the American Revolutionary War." Or perhaps instructors were told to explain the types of activities that they would engage in during the academic year—for example, "The teacher will discuss the key elements of the short-story form." Or, again, objectives might have been considered satisfactory even if they were stated in extremely loose terms, such as, "The student will gain a deep understanding of the underlying concepts of the physical sciences." All of these formulations of objectives were probably helpful to some degree; certainly they gave a general idea of what was to be covered, what was to be done by the teacher, or what the student was to learn. *However, they provided no explicit guidance for the teacher, either with respect to the selection of instructional sequences or to the evaluation of those sequences.*

In order to provide such guidance, it is necessary for the professional teacher to describe his objectives in terms of measurable learner behaviors—that is, in terms of what the learner can do or how he will act at the conclusion of instruction. Objectives stated in this way will leave little doubt about what the teacher's instructional intentions are. You may note that terms such as *goals, objectives, aims,* and *intents* have been used interchangeably throughout this discussion. Some writers draw a distinction among the terms. Some, for example, use the term *goal* to refer to a broad instructional intention of the society, whereas *objective* refers to a classroom intention on the part of a particular teacher. In some discussions it may be necessary to draw these distinctions, but since our treatment centers primarily upon the improvement of instruction, we shall treat all of these terms as equivalents. More specifically, an instructional objective describes a future behavioral response in the learner's repertoire that the instructor plans to promote. Somewhat more loosely, an objective stated in these operational terms is merely a description of what the learner is to be like after instruction. For example, instructional objectives may refer to the kinds of *behaviors* the learner will be able to manifest after instruction that he could not manifest before, such as the ability to compute certain arithmetical operations satisfactorily. Or again, such objectives might refer to the kinds of *products* a learner could produce at the conclusion of instruction that he could not produce prior to that instruction, such as an essay on the causes of World War II, or an end table made in the wood shop. Or, moving somewhat away from the more common instructional objectives, an operational statement of goals could refer to the kinds of responses that a student would make to an anonymous self-report questionnaire designed to assess learner interests in certain activities.

The essential quality of an operationally stated instructional objective is that the response that reflects the satisfactory attainment of the objective is thoroughly explicated. There ought to be no difficulty with a properly stated objective in determining whether the learner can satisfactorily attain the objective. To illustrate, examine the following three objectives:

> The learner will appreciate the importance of free speech in a democratic society.

The learner will be able to solve any pair of simultaneous equations involving two unknowns.
The learner will know what constitutes a good essay.

Which of the above objectives most clearly communicates an instructional intention, that is, which provides the least ambiguity with respect to what the teacher is attempting to accomplish? A moment's examination should convince you that the second objective, the objective that deals with the learner's solution of simultaneous equations, is the one that is least ambiguous. The trouble with the other two objectives is that they use elusive terms such as "appreciate" and "know" to communicate their intentions.

The authors have tried the following pedagogical experiment in our classes. We offered the grade "A" to any student (without his having to attend classes or take examinations) who could describe a learner behavior that would *invariably* signify the appreciation of a subject, such as music or art. In spite of several valiant attempts on the part of the students, no "A" was ever given. The reason is that there is simply no known way of identifying in an individual learner an *overt* behavior that *without question* signifies an *internal* phenomenon such as the satisfaction derived from an encounter with music. You might think that one could use indices such as a person's purchasing records in a music store, attending concerts, or smiling rapturously during key moments of a symphony. However, all of these behaviors can have varied interpretations. Perhaps a young man buys records because he likes the salesgirl who is selling them or because it is the "in" thing for his circle of friends to have a good collection of records. Perhaps he attends the symphony for similar reasons. An inspection of the darkened upper rows in the Hollywood Bowl during evening concerts will reveal that some of the young couples attend to other pursuits than music appreciation. Perhaps a person smiles during key moments of the symphony because he is daydreaming. It is clear that one cannot tell with certainty whether an *individual* student appreciates music merely because he engages in any of the foregoing activities.

It is possible, however, on a probabilistic basis to determine whether *groups* of individuals appreciate music. For instance, it is probably safe to say that among those individuals who volitionally attend symphonic concerts at the Hollywood Bowl, there are sizable numbers of music appreciators. Furthermore, if it could be demonstrated that a majority of individuals from high school music appreciation classes became volitional attenders of concerts at the Hollywood Bowl, we might be able to say, "On the basis of the probabilities involved, our music appreciation classes are having a desirable impact on learners." This can be depicted graphically, as in Figure 3. However, such conclusions do not assert that music appreciation can be observed in any one *individual* student.

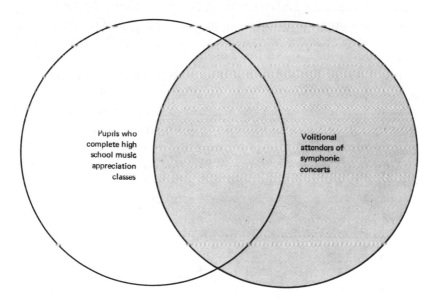

Figure 3. *Evaluating the Impact of Music Appreciation on a Probabilistic Basis*

The reason terms such as *appreciate, understand, know,* and *learn* have little value in the statement of instructional objectives is that they are too vague. One may draw from them, just as from a Rorschach ink blot, many divergent interpretations. Take a simple objective such as the following: "The student will know how to spell all of the three-letter words he has encountered during the first grade." One might think that with this relatively straightforward objective there would be certainty regarding its interpretation. Yet, think of the many ways in which the teacher could determine whether the student really "knows" the spelling of given words. The teacher could, for example, read the three-letter words aloud, and then have the learners write them down. This procedure is very common. On the other hand, he could present a list of words, some spelled correctly and some incorrectly, and have the learners select the correct ones. Or, again, he could orally present correct and incorrect spellings and ask the students to judge whether each word is properly or improperly spelled. Perhaps he could ask the youngsters to spell the words aloud. Maybe he could involve them in some kind of a "spelling bee," in which the children would judge the adequacy of their classmates' spelling of the words. Even with this very simple objective, we can see several ways in which it could be operationalized. The complex objective is usually much more susceptible to diverse interpretations. It is for this reason that we must state our objectives in operational terms—that is, in such a way that they describe how the learner will actually behave, or be able to behave, when he is finished with instruction.

Learner Behaviors and
Learner Products

When you stop to consider the kinds of techniques that a teacher can use to judge the degree to which a learner has achieved an instructional objective, there are really only two

ways of operationalizing goals: (1) we can describe the specific observable *behavior* in which the learner is to engage; or
(2) we can describe the kinds of *products* the learner will
produce. In the case of learner products we need not observe
his behavior, for we can subsequently examine the actual
product.

Turning first to learner behavior, you will note that there are
many activities in which learners engage that must be recorded
during the conduct of the activity. For example, if a student in
a speech class makes a presentation, we must record (such as
by means of a judge's rating form) the degree to which the
speech reached satisfactory levels of performance. If we fail
to make records of the speech performance, it is essentially
lost. If no one remembers how it was performed, a speech,
once made, disappears. It is the same as when a springboard
diver executes a complicated half gainer dive: if no one records
the dive during its operation, either through recording equipment (such as motion picture film) or a judge's evaluation, the
dive disappears in the pool. There are all sorts of learner behaviors that must be observed and recorded as they take place,
or else they vanish. Instances of learner behavior in common
teaching situations would be any kind of oral presentation
(such as panel reports, speeches, participation in discussion)
or athletic performance (running the hundred-yard dash, shooting basketball free throws, performing a high jump). All of
these learner behaviors must be recorded so that they can
be subsequently used for evaluation purposes. It is the teacher's responsibility in designing his instructional objectives not
only to explicate the kind of behavior the learner will engage
in, but also to develop a recording scheme so that records of
that behavior can subsequently be used for evaluation purposes.

In considering learner products, we can think of all sorts of
things the learner produces that we can subsequently evaluate.
For instance, any performance on a conventional test usually

produces some kind of answer sheet, essay response, or the like. These are instances of products the teacher can, at his leisure, evaluate well after they have been produced. Other instances of products might be the results of projects in home-making classes, typing classes, vocational education classes, and the like, where actual artifacts are produced by the learner. Of course, in the case of such products as a cheese soufflé there are limits (both sanitary and aesthetic) as to how long the teacher can retain the product for purposes of evaluation. But it is the learner product that is evaluated, not an observer's recording of a learner behavior.

This distinction between product and behavior may not at first seem necessary. However, some teachers work so predominantly with learner products that they fail to realize there are instances in which observations of certain learner behaviors will provide valuable indices of whether their instruction is effective. For instance, many social science teachers judge their learners' performance exclusively in terms of their test results or their term papers. There are other instances in which the observation (perhaps surreptitious) of learner performance in a largely unstructured group discussion might yield very worthwhile insights regarding the students' capacity to tolerate minority positions. Elementary school teachers, for example, may be interested in the degree of "self-confidence" that learners manifest. This behavior is often displayed in group situations requiring subtle and sophisticated observations on the part of the teacher. It is very difficult to get at nebulous notions such as self-confidence, but it is usually more valid to do so on an observational basis than by having the student write a theme on "My Self-Confidence."

Does Operationality Lead to Triviality?

A concern of many teachers when they first encounter operationally stated objectives is that such goals tend to be ex-

tremely trivial. It is only natural that many examples of operationally stated goals are relatively unimportant. The easiest
kinds of behavior to operationalize are the most simple. For
example, a teacher who is first given the charge to specify
an operationally stated goal dealing with the U.S. Senate might
readily turn to an objective such as the following: "The learner
will list in writing names of ten U.S. Senators." Such objectives
are easy to produce. Many beginners, unfortunately, stop with
such objectives, which describe only pedestrian kinds of behavior. But the very fact that objectives are stated operationally
allows us to identify those which are unimportant *and to discard them*. Few teachers want to teach the trivial, but many
teachers are now unconsciously doing it under the guise of
promoting the profound.

Suppose you were to ask a social science teacher what his
objective for the year was and he responded as follows: "My
goal is to make my students more sensitive to the importance
of functioning efficiently as citizens in a dynamic democracy."
You could do little to fault him. The objective sounds so
eminently worthwhile that no one could find much wrong with
it. The problem is, however, that this social science teacher
may at the end of the course assess his students, and by
implication, assess his instruction, with a simple true-false test.
In other words, the profundity of his objective tends to obfus-
cate the truly trivial nature of his assessment procedures. With
operationally stated goals, if we do tend toward trivia, at least
we can identify it and hopefully work toward something better.
There is no question that the statement of important objectives
in operational terms is difficult. But consider the following
hypothetical objective from an elementary statistics course:

> When presented with hypothetical descriptions of research
> design problems, the student will be able to select correctly
> from all of the statistical procedures treated in class that tech-
> nique most appropriate for the treatment of the data in the
> research problem.

It does not seem likely that this objective could be classified as trivial. Any student who could perform this objective must be in command of a number of skills, such as thorough familiarity with the statistical procedures treated in the class, conversance with the criteria that dictate when one technique should be used over another, and so on. The objective, however, is stated operationally. Both the learner and the teacher have a clear idea of what type of test will be given at the end of the course: hypothetical research design problems will be presented; the student will be asked to select the appropriate statistical analytic technique. If he can do it, he has achieved the objective. If he can't, he hasn't, and the teacher's instruction must be judged deficient. There is, in other words, no confusion about what the intention is, nor is there any ambiguity about whether the students can achieve the goal. As indicated, the objective is not trivial. Rather than promoting the trivial, the statement of objectives in operational form permits the teachers to identify unimportant goals, eliminate them and seek higher quality instructional objectives.

Selecting Appropriate Educational Objectives

There are at least two standards that a teacher might use to select appropriate, rather than unimportant, instructional objectives. It has been pointed out that to the degree that an instructional system is ineffective, we need not be too concerned with the quality of its instructional goals. However, to the extent that any system becomes capable of modifying learner behavior, we have to make sure that we are teaching the right things. Accordingly, our concern with the quality of our goals should be proportional to the quality of our instructional efforts. Since we are taking the position in this volume that systematic efforts can markedly improve the quality of instruction, it follows that we ought to be extremely concerned about the quality of our goals. A more elaborate consideration of the questions associated with the selection of goals will be provided in the next chapter.

Teacher Value Preferences

One criterion of overriding importance in the selection of instructional objectives is a teacher's value system regarding the content to be treated and the learner behaviors he hopes will emerge in connection with that content. Almost any teacher has his own conception of what *ought* to be done in his field. Secondary school teachers, strongly associated with particular subject disciplines, usually have fairly firm commitments to certain content or competencies in connection with their subject fields. For example, few historians can approach the whole field of history neutrally. They almost always have their favorite fields and subfields within the broader discipline, and they usually have a rough idea of what they want their students to know at the conclusion of the course. Similarly, elementary school teachers may have strong commitments toward certain kinds of learner behaviors, whether in language arts or mathematics. And the teacher's value framework, although usually not examined carefully, is most influential in selecting objectives. A more systematic consideration of that value framework will be provided in the following chapter, which deals with curricular decisions.

A Taxonomic Analysis

One standard that may be used in the selection of appropriate educational objectives has been provided by Professor Benjamin S. Bloom and his associates in connection with their work on the taxonomies of educational objectives.[1] In the early

[1]Benjamin S. Bloom (ed.), *Taxonomy of Educational Objectives, Handbook I: Cognitive Domain* (New York: David McKay Co., Inc., 1956). David R. Krathwohl, Benjamin S. Bloom, and Bertram B. Masia, *Taxonomy of Educational Objectives, Handbook II: Affective Domain* (New York: David McKay Co., Inc., 1964).

1950's Bloom and a group of his colleagues, primarily college examiners, attempted to set down the kinds of objectives that were commonly being measured in the schools at that time. As a consequence of their analysis, they divided the many objectives treated in the schools into three categories, or as they refer to them, domains. These were the *cognitive domain*, the *affective domain*, and the *psychomotor domain*. The cognitive domain is concerned with the intellectual responses of the learner, as made in performing mathematical solutions, composing an essay, or solving various kinds of "mental" problems. One might substitute "intellectual" or "cerebral" for "cognitive" and describe these kinds of learner behaviors satisfactorily. The affective domain concerns the attitudinal, emotional, and valuing responses of the learner; they are usually classified as interests, attitudes, appreciations, and the like. The psychomotor domain concerns the physical responses of the learner, as made in performing certain types of manipulative operations, athletic endeavors, and so on.

When the first taxonomy of educational objectives text (*Handbook I: Cognitive Domain*) appeared in 1956, it created a mild stir among educators, but certainly not an overwhelming flood of interest. It was not until several years later in the early 1960's that, as we indicated earlier, interest in the instructional objectives question really began to mount. About that time the second handbook, dealing with the affective domain, was published under the direction of Professor David Krathwohl. Undoubtedly the appearance of the second volume reinforced interest in the initial taxonomy. At any rate, one significant contribution of these two volumes is that they focused attention on the fact that very few teachers were attempting to achieve objectives in the affective domain. An analysis of the kinds of test items and observation procedures that were being used led one to the conclusion that the vast majority of instructional objectives in the schools were in the cognitive domain. Certainly there were those fields such as physical education, typing, or metal crafts in which psychomotor objectives dominated; but in the bulk of school subjects, such as the social sciences, language arts, the sciences, and so on, almost no affective objectives would ordinarily be found.

These taxonomies provide a helpful standard by which teachers can evaluate the quality of their objectives. Are they inadvertently overemphasizing the cognitive domain to the exclusion of the affective? There is nothing wrong with having objectives exclusively in the cognitive domain, if this is a rational choice by the teacher. The trouble is, however, that many teachers often unconsciously overemphasize the cognitive domain without realizing it. One of the values of these taxonomies is that they raise this important question of emphasis on one or another domain.

Some critics have rejected the value of the objectives taxonomies on the grounds that they attempt to separate into particular categories learner behaviors that are actually inseparable. These critics point out that human behavior is not exclusively a cognitive, affective, or psychomotor function, but a complicated melding of all three domains. While this assertion may be correct, it seems to us that a teacher is at least somewhat advantaged by thinking about learner behaviors in terms of being *primarily* in the affective, cognitive, or psychomotor domain. With such a consideration, it seems possible to survey more rigorously the quality of a set of instructional objectives.

Within each of the domains there are levels, probably hierarchical—although there is some equivocation regarding this point—that attempt to categorize different kinds of learner behavior within each of the domains. One of the problems here, however, is that the levels within the domains that Bloom and his associates have developed deal with essentially internal phenomena. A given overt response might be used, depending upon the situation in which it occurs, to represent very different kinds of internal learner responses. Take, for example, a pupil's selection of an alternative in a multiple-choice question. If he has previously seen the question, the selection may signify a very low level learner behavior involving the recall of that which is already learned. The very same action might signify a much higher level of learner behavior if the pupil has not previously encountered the question. In other words, the identical overt action may be used to represent different kinds of internal operations. This makes the attribution of objectives to different levels within the taxonomies very difficult, no matter what the domain. However at the very least the various levels within the domains would seem to have some heuristic value, in that they may cause the teachers to try to generate objectives that appear to get at higher levels of learner behaviors. Therefore, although it is not necessary to become very skilled at classifying behaviors into one category or another, for this task is extremely difficult and perhaps unprofitable, brief summaries of the levels within each domain will be presented below.

The Cognitive Domain

The cognitive domain has six levels. They move from knowledge, the lowest level, to evaluation, the highest level.

KNOWLEDGE.   Knowledge involves the recall of specifics or universals, the recall of methods and processes, or the recall of a pattern, structure, or setting. It will be noted that the essential attribute at this level is *recall*. For assessment purposes, a recall situation involves little more than "bringing to mind" appropriate material.

COMPREHENSION.   This level represents the lowest form of understanding and refers to a kind of apprehension that indicates that a student knows what is being communicated and can make use of the material or idea without necessarily relating it to other material or seeing it in its fullest implications.

APPLICATION.   Application involves the use of abstractions in particular or concrete situations. The abstractions used may be in the form of procedures, general ideas, or generalized methods. They may also be ideas, technical principles, or theories that must be remembered and applied.

ANALYSIS.   Analysis involves the breakdown of a communication into its constituent parts such that the relative hierarchy within that communication is made clear, that the relations beween the expressed ideas are made explicit, or both. Such analyses are intended to clarify the communication, to indicate how it is organized and the way in which the communication manages to convey its effects as well as its basis and arrangement.

SYNTHESIS.   Synthesis represents the combining of elements and parts so that they form a whole. This operation involves the process of working with pieces, parts, elements, and so on, and arranging them so as to constitute a pattern or structure not clearly present before.

EVALUATION.   Evaluation requires judgments about the value of material and methods for given purposes. Quantitative and qualitative judgments are made about the extent to which material and methods satisfy criteria. The criteria employed may be those determined by the learner or those given to him.

Most of the above levels, very briefly described here, have been broken down into various subcategories. For example, under evaluation there are two categories that deal with "judgments in terms of internal evidence" and "judgments in terms of external criteria." The knowledge category has twelve separate subdivisions. As indicated earlier, there would seem to be little utility in having a teacher become conversant with these subdivisions. It is probably sufficient if the teacher simply divides the cognitive taxonomy into (a) the lowest level, that is, knowledge, and (b) all those levels higher than the lowest, that is, comprehension through evaluation. Even this rough, two-category scheme will allow a teacher to identify the proportion of his objectives that fall into the lowest level category. And this seems to be the most important advantage of the cognitive taxonomy—namely, encouraging the teacher to identify what proportion of his objectives are at the very lowest level. Unfortunately, far too many of the objectives currently used in the schools require only recall on the part of the learner and can be aptly classified as merely knowledge objectives. There is nothing intrinsically wrong with knowledge, but if this is all we are asking of students, we probably should set our sights somewhat higher.

The Affective Domain

The affective domain is subdivided into five levels. These levels in particular may cause the teacher much difficulty in classifying objectives. Once more, these levels may have some value in that they encourage the teacher to think about different forms of objectives, but it is not recommended that the teacher devote too much time in attempting to classify various objectives within these levels.

RECEIVING (Attending).   The first level of the affective domain is concerned with the learner's sensitivity to the existence of certain phenomena and stimuli, that is, with his willingness to receive or to attend to them. This category is divided into three subdivisions that indicate three different levels of attending to phenomena—namely, awareness of the phenomena, willingness to receive phenomena, and controlled or selected attention to phenomena.

RESPONDING.   At this level one is concerned with responses that go beyond merely attending to phenomena. The student is sufficiently motivated that he is not just "willing to attend," but is actively attending.

VALUING.   This category reflects the learner's holding of a particular value. The learner displays behavior with sufficient consistency in appropriate situations that he actually is perceived as holding this value.

ORGANIZATION. As the learner successively internalizes values, he encounters situations in which more than one value is relevant. This requires the necessity of organizing his values into a system such that certain values exercise greater control.

CHARACTERIZATION BY A VALUE OR VALUE COMPLEX. At this highest level of the affective taxonomy internalization has taken place in an individual's value hierarchy to the extent that we can actually characterize him as holding a particular value or set of values.

The definitions for the affective taxonomy are clearly far less rigorous than for those of the cognitive taxonomy, and those who work with the cognitive taxonomy often suggest that these affective levels need much more precision. Both of these taxonomies have been presented, however, because they are in common use today, and it may be that if the teacher becomes more familiar with them he will find them of some utility. While an extensive reading of the original taxonomies is not necessary, some teachers may find this a useful enterprise.

The Psychomotor Domain

Bloom, Krathwohl, and their associates have not yet developed a taxonomy in the psychomotor domain. One is available, however, and has received some attention in recent months. This system, by E. J. Simpson,[2] will be briefly summarized here.

PERCEPTION. The first step in performing a motor act is the process of becoming aware of objects, qualities, or relations

[2]E. J. Simpson, "A Slightly Tongue-in-Cheek Device for Teacher Cogitation," *Illinois Teacher of Home Economics*, X, No. 4 (Winter 1966–1967).

by way of the sense organs. It is the main portion of the situation-interpretation-action chain leading to motor activity.

SET. Set is a preparatory adjustment for a particular kind of action or experience. Three distinct aspects of set have been identified—namely, mental, physical, and emotional.

GUIDED RESPONSE. This is an early step in the development of a motor skill. The emphasis is upon the abilities that are components of the more complex skill. Guided response is the overt behavioral act of an individual under the guidance of another individual.

MECHANISM. At this level the learner has achieved a certain confidence and degree of skill in the performance of an act. The habitual act is a part of his repertoire of possible responses to stimuli and the demands of situations where the response is appropriate.

COMPLEX OVERT RESPONSE. At this level, the individual can perform a motor act that is considered complex because of the movement pattern required. The act can be carried out efficiently and smoothly, that is, with minimum expenditure of energy and time.

Measures in the Affective Domain

As we indicated previously, one of the grave dangers in stating objectives in operational terms is that the teacher may succumb to the tendency to aim toward only trivial behaviors. By using a carefully examined value system, coupled with a taxonomic analysis of learner behavior, the teacher should be able to avoid this pitfall.

Measures in the affective domain are particularly difficult to develop. Whereas the cognitive domain asks the question "What *can* the learner do?" the affective domain poses the question

"What *will* the learner do?" This means that the teacher must become very ingenious at devising evaluation situations in which the learner is permitted to behave with almost no cues from the teacher. For example, if he is concerned with the degree to which students are interested in his subject field, he cannot very well ask them, "How many of you like this course?" Obviously any thinking student who is concerned about a good grade will raise his hand. Even anonymous, self-report devices have the same limitation in that the seasoned student will realize that a collection of unsigned yet negative responses from the class may incline a teacher to view the whole group of students unfavorably and produce low grades for all students.

It may be advantageous to think of situations in which the learner is responding to natural rather than teacher-manipulated stimuli. If, for example, it is possible to observe how a pupil behaves when he is not aware that he is being observed, one has a much better estimate of how he really feels than if the learner is clearly behaving for the teacher's benefit. Whereas measures in the lower levels of the cognitive domain are relatively simple to construct, measures in the affective domain are usually very difficult to devise. This difficulty can be illustrated with an actual account of how we attempted to develop a measure of our students' attitude toward an instructional model similar to the one being advocated in this volume.[3] We had discovered in a teacher-preparation course that we were able to get relatively high learner performance on cognitive measures. We were also anxious to discover the degree to which students manifested positive attitudes toward the instructional model, so we developed a series of twelve fictitious instructional problems and for each of them presented four solutions, thereby producing 48 responses in all. Only about half of these solutions were really germane to the instructional

[3]W. James Popham and Eva L. Baker, *Validation of an Inventory Measuring Attitudes Toward Instructional Principles*. Cooperative Research Project No. S-069, Office of Education, U.S. Department of Health, Education, and Welfare, June, 1965.

model we were concerned with; the rest of the alternatives were simply there for camouflage. We asked our students to rate each of the 48 responses on a five-point scale from highly inappropriate to highly appropriate. We were concerned only with the responses to the items relevant to the instructional model. Student performance on this instrument, therefore, represented what we hoped would be an affective response to the instructional model we were advocating. The problem was to provide a situation that would allow us to determine whether responses to this instrument represented anything more than answering for the teacher's benefit.

Accordingly, we arranged a situation with a colleague in which he would solicit students for an "extra credit" project in which they could earn extra credit in our course by participating as "conventional" teachers in a study contrasting (a) teaching machines versus (b) "ordinary" teachers. In an effort to heighten their motivation, our students were informed that the teaching-machine manufacturer had said, "No human teacher can out-perform my machine." They were told that they would be going to the university laboratory school to instruct sixth-grade pupils and that no other person would be present in the room to observe them. They were asked to teach a particular lesson in the field of sociology by any procedure they wished, but to teach it as well as they could in view of the contrast of conventional versus the teaching-machine instruction. During two semesters, well over 100 of our students reported to the university laboratory school to participate in the study.

We had previously trained the sixth-grade pupils to become very adept observers in the use of our instructional model. After a ten- to fifteen-minute teaching situation in which our students taught these sixth-grade pupils, the pupils would return to us (located in a classroom removed from the scene of the experiment) to report the degree to which the teachers had used appropriate parts of our instructional model. The sixth graders became particularly adroit in observing the model and, via subsequent questionnaire evaluations, only one of approximately 100 of our teacher-preparation students suspected that the sixth grade pupils were accomplices. By correlating (a) the degree to which our students used this instructional model in a situation where they were supposedly unobserved and (b) their scores on our attitude inventory, we were able to establish the validity of the inventory. Fortunately, in this instance there was a positive correlation, and in the future we were therefore able to "teach to our test" instead of arranging the complex accomplice situation at the laboratory school. We have often wondered what the impact of that experiment will be upon the relations of those sixth grade pupils with their future teachers.

While one need not go to this much trouble to develop or validate an affective measuring instrument, it is certainly true that the preparation of those instruments takes far more time and trouble than do the simple cognitive measuring instruments that most teachers use. However, affective measures may get at the most important kinds of learner behaviors. Given a choice between having a student learn something specific about chemistry in the cognitive domain and having him learn to develop a scientific attitude, there seems to be little question as to which is more important. The difficulty in measuring such elusive attributes as "a scientific attitude" should not discourage a teacher's efforts to get at them.

Establishing Performance Standards

It is one thing to know *what* you want the student to do; it is another to know *how well* you want him to do it. One of the tasks facing the teacher is to determine the level of performance that he will expect from students on operationally stated objectives, once the objectives have been identified. There are two distinct questions to be answered here; one concerns the level of performance for a particular student, the other concerns the level of performance for a group of students (such as a class). The necessity of reaching both judgments is made clear when one considers the problems associated with the possible revision of an instructional sequence. Suppose a teacher identifies his objectives with great clarity, designs and carries out an instructional sequence, and at the end of the sequence measures pupil performance. How can he decide whether the students have performed well enough that he need not revise the instructional sequence? If he delays the establishment of performance standards until after instruction, there will be a tendency to give himself "the benefit of the doubt" and to assume the students have done just about as well as they could. It is more difficult to establish, in advance of instruction, how well he thinks the student will do, then push toward this standard. Even though it is difficult, the tactic of setting performance standards in advance of instruction usually forces the teacher to set higher levels of performance.

Student Minimal Levels

In the first place, the teacher must indicate the level of proficiency that he expects of a particular student. For example, if he wants students to perform certain division operations involving three-digit numbers, he ought to state what proportion of the problems on the final examination the student will be able to solve correctly. For example, should he be able to solve 85 per cent of the problems correctly, or should he be able to solve all of them correctly? In many cases, the teacher will set a student proficiency level somewhat lower than 100 per cent to allow for calculation errors, casual oversights, carelessness, and so on. On the other hand, there are instances in which the teacher expects 100 per cent proficiency from the students, and this too should be specified.

There are some situations in which the standard of student proficiency is strongly dictated by the educational experiences that will follow. For example, if a teacher is conducting an introductory class in algebra that is to be followed by advanced algebra classes, he may have definite indications regarding the level of proficiency that the subsequent teacher will expect of his students. This expectation can aid him to a considerable extent in establishing student performance levels. On the other hand, it is more commonly the case that the teacher will have to be guided by his own experience regarding how well students should do. A beginning teacher, of course, may have far more difficulty here than an experienced teacher. Even so, as soon as possible he should carefully analyze what levels of proficiency the student ought to be able to display at a given unit of instruction and then, at least tentatively, describe those standards.

Class Minimal Levels

In addition to establishing student minimal levels, the teacher ought to describe how well the total class should perform with respect to the objective. For example, he might indicate that 90 per cent of the class ought to perform with at least 80 per cent proficiency on the sentence-analysis exercises in the final examination. Or, again, all of the students should be able to recite from memory, with no more than one error, the five-line passages indicated in the text. It is important to establish class minimal levels in addition to student minimal levels because it will be on this basis that the teacher can decide whether to revise an instructional sequence. Student minimal levels are particularly useful in identifying individuals who may need remedial instruction. Class minimal levels are helpful in determining whether a sequence of instruction should be revised.

As we indicated earlier, it is very difficult for beginning teachers to establish minimal levels, and they perhaps should not make the attempt until they have taught for a year or two. However, as soon as they have experience and realize what can be expected from students, they should set their student and class minimal levels. Perhaps they should set standards higher than the performance they have already been getting from their learners and attempt to achieve these augmented levels of proficiency.

There was a time when the U.S. Air Force had established 90–90 criterion levels of proficiency for their instructional materials. The Air Force would not allow certain kinds of instructional materials to be used until 90 per cent of the students taking the examination passed with a proficiency level of 90 per cent or better on the examination. This system is, of course, somewhat deceptive, since one can achieve a 90–90 criterion level simply by lowering the difficulty level of the test involved, but it does provide some rough guidelines for the preparation of the instructional materials.

Examine the objective below and note that the student minimal level section of the objective is in italic, whereas the class minimal level section of the objective is in boldface type. It is toward this type of objective that the teacher, after some experience, should strive.

> At the end of the course **at least 80 per cent of the students** should be able to conjugate correctly *at least 90 per cent* of any regular "ie" verb in the Spanish language.

The establishment of performance standards is very complicated. Sometimes there will be external criteria to guide the teacher, so that he knows he is pushing toward, for example, 100 per cent proficiency. On other occasions the standards are far more nebulous. In cases of cognitive objectives, it may be that we can hold individual students to a particular level of proficiency, whereas in cases of affective consequences it is probably more realistic to talk about a total class performance rather than about the performance of individual learners.

The relationship of the assignment of grades to pupils and performance standards will be examined in Chapter 9. At this point, however, it should be pointed out that we are here concerned primarily with performance standards for *the quality of instruction*, not for giving grades to individual learners. It is by using these performance standards that a teacher can establish whether his instruction has been adequate.

The Target Population
of Learners

In defining objectives with complete operationality, in the proper domain, and with sophisticated performance standards, it is always necessary to consider the target population of learners. The objectives that one might establish for a group of youngsters in a thoroughly advantaged, upper socio-economic level school would obviously be different from those that would be established for youngsters who are forced to scratch out an education in a subculture thoroughly resistant to the advantages of schooling. The wise teacher will modify his objectives to be consistent with the target group of youngsters with whom he must deal.

Instructional Objectives
as the Key

We have given considerable attention to the topic of instructional objectives because they represent one of the most important tools available to the teacher. The more clearheaded the teacher is about what he is attempting to accomplish with his learners, the more easily he can accomplish it and the more readily he can judge whether he has accomplished it. There is undoubtedly a positive relationship between a teacher's clarity of instructional goals and the quality of his teaching. To the degree that a teacher is uncertain about what he is attempting to accomplish with learners, and to the degree that those objectives are not worth achieving, there will be poor instructional results.

We should not, however, underemphasize the difficulty of stating objectives rigorously. It is far easier to walk into a classroom and just "start teaching" than to think about what you want to have learners become as a consequence of instruction. But even though the stating of objectives is difficult, it is important to do so, for the students suffer from a lack of teacher clarity regarding goals. The first step in a systematic approach to instruction is unquestionably the specification of objectives in operational terms.

ADDITIONAL READING

Bloom, Benjamin S. (ed.), *Taxonomy of Educational Objectives, Handbook I: Cognitive Domain* (New York: David McKay Co., Inc., 1956).

Eisner, E. W., "Educational Objectives: Help or Hindrance?" *School Review*, LXXV, No. 3 (1967).

Krathwohl, David R., Benjamin S. Bloom, and Bertram B. Masia, *Taxonomy of Educational Objectives, Handbook II: Affective Domain* (New York: David McKay Co., Inc., 1964).

Mager, Robert F., *Preparing Instructional Objectives* (Palo Alto, Calif.: Fearon Publishers, Inc., 1962).

Payne, David A., *The Specification and Measurement of Learning Outcomes* (Waltham, Mass.: Blaisdell Publishing Co., 1968).

4

Curricular Decisions

"Curriculum" is a Latin-based word that evokes in many teachers the same enthusiasm as "polemics" does in an activist. "Curriculum," teachers may feel, is usually formulated on the school-district level by phantom consultants. It is then duly printed in a thick curriculum guide that no one except a probationary teacher bothers to consult. Perhaps to traditional teachers, curriculum as a field of inquiry is beside the point; but to teachers who wish to make rational decisions in their classrooms, an understanding of curriculum is vital.

Curricular concerns have to do with *which* objectives the teacher seeks to implement. A laissez-faire attitude toward this question was tolerable in earlier epochs of education because our generalizable knowledge about instruction was relatively scant. Interest in the source of objectives in a classroom becomes more important when the instructional process is more efficient. Once we have demonstrated that we can teach certain concepts effectively, attention is diverted to the question of what *should* be taught. We are at that point now.

There is a certain "oughtness" associated with curriculum

questions, since the selection of the objectives of instruction is subjective. There are no schemes to depersonalize it completely, and in fact it is the teacher, not impersonal outside agents, who actually controls the curriculum. The teacher can almost always select the specific objectives he feels important for his students to achieve. Of course, school districts, curriculum guides, state departments of education, school department chairmen, and principals exert influence on the teacher's choices. But the teacher makes the final decision.

It is imperative that the teacher's decision be rational. He should use all available data when he decides what the classroom curriculum will be for his students. Unfortunately, some teachers overlook sources of objectives available to them. They don't renounce certain kinds of objectives, they simply lose them by default. For example, suppose you are a teacher and you wish to adhere closely to district policy and implement the objectives generally subscribed to by the administrative hierarchy. What will confront you is a curriculum guide that in most cases exhaustively describes *content* areas for you to teach. Usually the objectives are nonbehavioral; that is, they do not describe observable acts or products of the learners. Instead, a list of specific learning activities might be described, supposedly designed to bring about the general objectives. Teachers in such situations may often look to the textbook for confirmation of the curriculum guide's outline. The areas where the two coincide may prescribe, more or less, the limits of the objectives. Such a set of goals typically deals with subject matter almost exclusively, since that is the focus of textbooks. Any other kinds of objectives are ignored. Although his instructional plan is not very clear at this point, a teacher may feel generally comfortable in this position. He feels he has done what was expected in the way of "mapping out the course."

Another teacher may similarly obtain a set of subject-matter objectives, but his process and motivation may be entirely different. This teacher does not wish to conform to the dictates of the curriculum guide, and finds available texts inadequate, inappropriate, and in error. He may question the academic credentials of the guidebook writer. This teacher feels he is an expert in his subject-matter area and decides not to water down the curriculum he presents. The primary sources of his objectives are his college texts and notes. Aside from the instructional problems a teacher of this type generally encounters, he has forfeited a huge area of potential classroom objectives, and his curriculum is often lopsided.

A third teacher engages in curriculum building in a much different fashion; he feels that only through the children's determination of the objectives can learning become a meaningful experience, so he does not plan his instruction in advance. Rather, he subtly guides his students' interest by providing alluring materials for them to inspect. In this way they may pursue those topics that intrigue them.

These three examples are not supplied as parodies. They represent, somewhat baldly, the kinds of curriculum generation common to many teachers. Because these teachers usually keep their objectives "in their heads" rather than putting them down on paper, they may be only dimly aware of how they are selecting what they wish to have happen to their students. Our position is not that a satisfactory curriculum must demonstrate "three of these kinds of objectives and two of another"; rather, our desire is to promote the teacher's conscious perception of many of the factors contributing to his curricular decisions. Certainly this perception can never be complete; but if a teacher does attempt to explore the curricular options available to him and decides exactly *what* he wishes to teach and *why* he wishes to teach it, he will be in a better position to justify the time he spends in the classroom.

The Curriculum

Because curriculum is subjective, there is a tendency for some to attempt esoteric definitions of the term. For academic disputation, such an endeavor may be satisfying. A simple definition, however, could be: *Curriculum is all the planned learning outcomes for which the school is responsible.* Notice the inclusion of "planned." Other learnings may occur by chance and probably will, but these may not be taken account of in the teacher's plan. It seems reasonable to worry only about that which you can control, and it is next to impossible to control that which isn't even anticipated. The second notable characteristic of the definition is the focus on "outcomes." Curriculum definitions that refer to "experiences" of the learner seem to muddle up the means-ends distinction that makes curriculum reasonably investigatable. The curriculum refers to the desired consequences of instruction. Therefore, using tests as measures of *outcomes* might better exemplify what *is* the curriculum than a list of texts or materials used in instruction.

The distinction between ends and means is not difficult to make, and can help the teacher greatly in his instructional planning. For one thing, the decisions regarding objectives— the ends of instruction—almost always depend on value judgments about what the schools *should* teach—that is, what is *important* for the students to learn. Value judgments, however, should contribute only mildly, if at all, to decisions about *how* the objectives can best be attained. When goals are established, the efficiency of comparative instructional techniques, or means, can be evaluated empirically. As yet, systematic empirical verification of the quality of educational objectives is nearly impossible.

A Framework for the Selection of Objectives

Ralph Tyler has provided a great deal of important material on the curriculum in his writings. He offers a comprehensive model for justifying the selection of educational ends. The purpose of using such a model is to encourage the teacher or curriculum writer to take account of relevant sources of data in the derivation of his objectives. Tyler (1950) suggests the use of three major sources of data from which objectives may be constructed: the *learner*, the *society*, and the *subject-matter discipline*. As seems to be true with every other topic in the social sciences, these categories are neither mutually exclusive nor totally exhaustive. However, within each is a body of data sufficiently unique to justify the classificatory scheme. Tentative objectives selected from each of these three major areas are to be examined with respect to one's philosophical position and to what is known about the psychology of learning. Uses of philosophy and psychology enter in all phases of the process, but a final check seems desirable. Objectives that are found to be consistent with the "screens" of *philosophy of education* and *psychology of learning* are next phrased in operational terms. A rational curriculum should be the end result. Tyler's procedure—the model that he advocates—can be used at almost any level of instructional generality—for the selection of a K-12 set of objectives, a year-long curriculum, or a teaching unit of a month's duration. Each of the sections of Tyler's rationale will now be considered in more detail.

The Learner

The learner—the high school student or the first grade child—is the first basic data source of possible objectives. We should have some idea of the abilities of the learner so that we can decide what he is likely to know already. In addition, we might use the learner's own interests and needs as a basis for certain curricular decisions. Where the purposes of the school seem largely irrelevant to the students, the problem can often be traced to the omission of the *learner* as a source of educational objectives. For example, in many low-income, urban schools much of what happens instructionally by-passes the students because it seems too academic and too far removed from the things that concern them. Teachers who have been successful and have felt rewarded by their teaching efforts often allow the children's areas of concern to help guide what is taught. How does one find out what the students are interested in learning? Tyler suggests some major avenues to answer this question. The first is for the teacher to interview the students himself, to ask the children directly what they think they should be doing. This method is definitely straightforward and assumes that the students will trust the teacher enough to be honest, which is likely if he and the students come from the same milieu and share a set of fairly consonant values. When there is a great discrepancy between the teacher's background and the students' environment, it may be difficult to achieve the necessary openness. He could, of course, ask students to complete questionnaires in order to help him find out more about them. If so, it would seem wiser to ask questions like "What do you like to do?" rather than "What do you want to learn?" since the second question sounds rather "teachery" and may elicit answers reflecting what the students think the teacher wants to hear.

Interviewing or using questionnaires may be difficult, especially with young children. To gather useful information the teacher must also learn to observe the students carefully. He may have to drop his teacher-pupil perspective and look at them as individual people. By observing students' out-of-school interests, and by conversing with other teachers, the teacher can determine what it is that really concerns the students. Of course, extensive teaching experience is a great help and, for this reason, the novice teacher often has trouble in selecting learner-based objectives.

It is also helpful for the teacher to try to remember, if he can, what it was like to be twelve (if this is the age of his pupils). This approach is probably of little value in general, because what he was like at the age of his students is dramatically different from what students of the same age are like now.

For example, students today are investigating the use of power and dissent to a much greater degree than students ever have in the past. Forces impinge on today's child that didn't affect the teacher at all. If he tries to remember what it was like to be six or seven, his memory is likely to fail, or he will recall a stylized version of himself, largely colored by parental reminiscences. However, such recollections are better than nothing in getting a fix on his students' probable interests.

Another source of data about the learner is reposited in the writing of educational psychologists. For instance, proponents of Piaget[1] might feel that children are unable to perform particular skills until they reach certain ages. Yet there is so much controversy about early childhood developmental patterns that it is a little dangerous to view any of these writings as unimpeachable sources of truth. Psychology, and even psychoanalytic theory, can also be used as sources for objectives. The writings of Havighurst[2] and Erikson[3] may be sources of this type of learner data.

After the teacher has gathered data about the learner's needs or interests, how does he transform this information into an objective? In some cases, it is not too difficult. Suppose he finds that 70 per cent of his students would like to learn about Negro history. An objective in a history class might be easily generated:

> The students will be able to describe in an essay the contribution of six prominent Negro politicians in the twentieth century.

If he teaches an English class and gathers the same data—that is, that 70 per cent of his students are interested in Negro

[1]Jean Piaget and Barbel Inhelder, *The Early Growth of Logic in the Child, Classification and Seriation* (New York: Harper & Row, Publishers, 1964).

[2]Havighurst, R., *Human Development and Education* (New York: Longmans, Green & Company, Ltd., 1953).

[3]Erikson, E. H., *Childhood and Society* (New York: W. W. Norton & Company, Inc., Publishers, 1950).

history, the conversion of the data to a usable objective within his classroom is possible. Many English teachers, upon learning that their students are interested in history, would conclude that the problem belonged to the social science department and abdicate responsibility for it. However, objectives that take account of this data source and are reasonable for use in an English class might be:

1. The students will prepare a ten-minute speech, using X and Y techniques, discussing a prominent Negro in American politics.

2. The student will write a 500-word essay with a topic sentence, development by example, and a concluding statement. The topic of the essay will be Negro contributions to the culture of the United States.

It should be obvious that learners' interests and needs are not necessarily limited to a teacher's subject-matter field. In departmentalized teaching, whether in elementary, secondary, or higher education, the subject-matter organization can tend to reduce the cognizance teachers take of students' needs or interests outside the subject matter.

Another example might be helpful. Suppose there is information which suggests that children should learn to delay gratifications. Perhaps it is discovered that if children can work for a time without extrinsic rewards, the children will be able to adjust better to a complex environment. Such information is not linked to any traditional subject-matter field, but an objective dealing with these data could be effectively implemented in reading, arithmetic, music, or any subject-matter discipline. When curricula are dominated by the learner as a source of objectives, they may be given the "progressive" label with all its sometimes negative connotations. But it is obvious to anyone who ever learned anything that learning becomes more exciting when one is vitally concerned with the goals that have been selected. There is much evidence in the literature of behavioral science that this is so. The student-operated "experimental colleges," where learners design and implement the objectives they want without the necessary reward of grades and course credit, are a contemporary example of the power of a learner-centered curriculum. However, the learner is just one of three sources for objectives in Tyler's model.

The Society

Certainly, our society has expectations for its schools. To employ the customary clichés, society expects the production of "good citizens," properly "versed in the culture," and able "to function in the social environment." Some might also add that masses of these "products" ought not to leave school before they are 17 or 18 unless we wish to provoke an economic disaster. The data that societal expectations supply can be a potent source of operational school objectives rather than merely a basis for educational platitudes.

What are some of these societal objectives? How is it possible to prepare students to live in a future society that no one can currently define? The questions are difficult, yet we can begin to make progress in answering them. For example, if we do know that our society will be changing rapidly, an objective might be to help the student learn to cope with change—that is, to be able to react appropriately to given changes in his environment. This ability could be measured in situational tests where markedly different conditions were provided for the performance of a set of tasks.

The area of "good citizenship" is another concern that reflects a commitment to societal objectives. The problem with "good citizenship" goals is the inherent difficulty one has in assessing this type of aim. Still, it is possible to describe a set of specific behaviors, such as the learner's observance of classroom rules and his volunteering to help other students, and then to stipulate that the student should demonstrate at least some of these actions.

The societal objectives briefly discussed so far are those derived from pervasive societal concerns that crosscut all subject fields. Within separate subject fields, however, objectives serving society's expectations could also be derived.

For example, many of the objectives of home-economics education, business education, and vocational training particularly reflect society's needs. The inclusion in public school curriculum of courses to train keypunch machine operators is a prominent example. In health classes the objectives relating to the dangers of drugs and tobacco are also societally derived. Certainly any job-training course is predicated (or should be) on the need for trained personnel that exists, or will exist, in the community.

In the more traditional disciplines, societal objectives are also often found. Units in English classes that deal with the impact of mass media, the distinction between fact and opinion, and the ability to write business letters and personal notes all relate to societal objectives, though some might reasonably contend that promoting skills in simple arithmetic operations is more relevant to society's needs than teaching the nature of mathematics.

How does a teacher decide what possible types of societal objectives are relevant for his students? Knowledge of the community in which the students live is requisite, as is keeping up with the changes predicated for the larger society. Sociological studies can also help in identifying the prevailing trends in the society. A close relationship between teachers and community public-service agencies can provide another valuable source of societal generalizations.

From a generalization such as "There is an increasing emphasis on storage-and-retrieval of information," an objective might merge such as "The student can, when given a task, quickly locate and identify the data source to which he should attend."

It is not necessary at this point to phrase objectives in staunchly operational terms. Rather, general objectives that broadly define the behavior and content expected can be economically used for the time being. Forming technically correct behavioral objectives is the last phase of the curriculum-building task.

**Subject Matter
as a Source**

The traditional source of the majority of classroom objectives is the subject-matter discipline in which the teacher is teaching. English classes have most of their objectives relating to English-type concepts. Biology teachers teach mostly biology. Yet the question shoud be raised, "From where do these subject-oriented teachers derive the concepts they teach?" The answer usually leads either to the textbooks and materials the teacher uses or to those concepts and collections of information acquired during his college training.

This is an unfortunate state of affairs, since texts are sometimes inadequate and colleges frequently parochial. The subject-related concepts a teacher uses in his instruction often do not reflect the best thought in the field. He may be laboring at the cutting edge of trivia. In teaching the humanities one is slightly better off if he sticks with what he learned about subject matter in college. But in the sciences, concepts are quickly obsolete and the teacher unwittingly teaches untruths. And even when the teacher is relatively sure that he is teaching accurate and up-to-date concepts, how can he choose which of the thousands of concepts in his field he should teach?

It has been suggested that a sensible approach to the problem is to identify the major ideas in one's field and attempt to generate objectives that exemplify them. If an English teacher is anxious to teach something about the grammar of the language, one important idea that could be taught concerns word order. To derive valid objectives, he would want to have students respond to the concept of word order. Similarly, in any scientific endeavor predominant characteristics are observation and objectivity. These two attributes should be reflected in objectives dealing with science.

We do not advocate the use of these "key concepts" as a basis for planning objectives in a given subject field merely because authorities say so. The identification of these pervasive and powerful concepts makes it seem reasonable that if these concepts are mastered, the student will have acquired the ability to relate his own thoughts to these key concepts. Thus the use of certain principles underlying a discipline helps the student collate and generalize the ideas in a single discipline. This is a much more efficient process than learning a vast number of interesting but discrete bits of information and dabs of principles without a strongly delineated structure in which to place them. The hope that the student will somehow arrive at these ideas himself is overly optimistic, slightly sadistic, and generally inefficient.

The three major sources for objectives according to Tyler are, as we have seen, the learner, the society, and the subject-matter discipline. The relationship of these sources to the taxonomic analyses of objectives may have occurred to you. It does seem clear that there are likely to be a great many subject-matter-derived objectives in the cognitive domain, since cognition deals with intellectual skills. But the relationship is by no means one-to-one. Certain subject-matter objectives may be psychomotor and some are affective—for instance, the consideration of how well the student likes the subject field. Similarly, many societal and learner objectives will relate to the affective domain, since demonstration of them—for example, tolerance for diversity, "good citizenship," and the like—may require voluntary acts that demonstrate preference and commitment rather than solely an intellectual understanding of the situation. Students can "understand" why hostility is bad but still be unwilling to curb its display. There are also many learner and societal objectives that are cognitive. This must be obvious since valuing behaviors are frequently demonstrated after certain cognitive learnings have taken place.

At this point in Tyler's scheme, the teacher or curriculum worker who has faithfully adhered to Tyler's guidelines has three sets of objectives, derived from the subject field, the learner, or the society. They may be stated rather generally at this point. There will undoubtedly be a fair amount of overlap as well as far too many objectives to use. And even if one could employ them all it would not be useful to do so, since objectives taken from three disparate sources may well be conflicting. How does one decide what his teaching objectives will finally be? Tyler suggests the imposition of two "screens" or sets of standards against which one can validate his objectives.

Screen One: Philosophy of Education

How does an educational philosophy help you make practical curricular decisions? And what is an educational philosophy? How many of us have very clearly stated philosophies of anything?

Educational philosophy should help you to decide if the objective *should* be taught. If your philosophical position is, generally speaking, that the school's primary function is to disseminate knowledge that has been transmitted through civilized cultures, this certainly would affect your judgment of certain objectives generated from the learner and societal sources. Probably many of the objectives based on individual needs and social desires could not be justified in terms of such a general philosophical position. If, on the other hand, your position were that the schools should attempt to promote the development of each individual's particular potential, then many objectives suggested by data about the society and the learner would be retained.

A principal purpose in applying the philosophical screen is to reduce the chance that objectives will conflict with one another. But it should be clear that we are using the term "philosophy" in a rather liberal fashion, and it is not implied that in order to write objectives, one must have a well-formulated philosophy with Roman-numeral postulates and propositions. And in some cases, the philosophy used to screen objectives is really the general policy of the particular school district in which the teacher is employed. What is appropriate to teach may be defined by the board of education. It is also true that philosophy was operating to some extent back in the early stages of the Tyler model when the curriculum maker decided to go to X source to derive Z objective from the learner. But the explicit use of educational philosophy as a check on the worth and consistency of the objectives will usually reduce the number of objectives and result in a set of goals that, in the eyes of the teacher or curriculum worker, ought to be taught.

Screen Two: Psychology of Learning

As the number of objectives has been reduced by the use of a philosophical screen, the use of a screen relating to psychology of learning will generally result in a still smaller list. The psychological screen is used to ask if the objectives *can* be taught. Are they likely to be achieved within the structure of the schools as they currently exist and within the amount of time the teacher can expend on the objective? A set of statements regarding what changes can usually be achieved in classroom settings will indicate that certain objectives are very unrealistic.

An objective for secondary school students, for example, taken from a curriculum guide published by a state education department reads: "To be able to relate self-image to behavior." Without intensive clinical treatment the chances for the attainment of this objective are slim, and it ought to be deleted. Similarly, other objectives that promise major personality alterations should probably be omitted.

In addition, objectives that require the retention of great quantities of minute detail at the knowledge level of Bloom's cognitive taxonomy might well be deleted, since available evidence indicates that large numbers of facts are not well retained. Instructional time totally spent in promoting their acquisition, therefore, is generally wasted.

Sometimes implicit in the use of a particular psychology of learning is the selection of the method by which instruction takes place. Selection of certain methods—for example, the use of reinforcement—might increase the chance that particular objectives would be achieved, while other techniques might be appropriate for different objectives. The use of psychology of learning simply increases one's chances of designing a list of objectives that *can* be achieved.

Operational Objectives

The next step in the process of curriculum design is the precise description of the final set of objectives in operational terms. First of all this means that the type of student behavior to be demonstrated must be clearly described. In addition, the population of content to which the behavior will apply should be stated. Ideally, the behavior should apply to a large, rather than to a small, body of content. An objective such as, "Given any Elizabethan lyric, the student will write a description of the author's purpose and theme," is better than, "Given 'To Althea From Prison' the student will write a description of the author's purpose and theme." The reason the first objective is better is that it applies more generally to a greater body of knowledge. The broader the *content generality* of an objective, the more useful it ordinarily is.

Objectives should also be checked to see that they are not exclusively at the knowledge level of the cognitive taxonomy but that they require the student to process and *use* knowledge as well as to recall it. Attention should also be paid to the number of affective objectives selected, to ensure against unintentioned planning of only cognitive goals. Levels of pupil performance expected can also be added where possible. If all the above steps are followed, you should have a set of objectives that was formed by the widest possible survey of existing needs and demands, objectives that are internally consistent and that *should* be achieved according to an explicit (if primitive) philosophical position, and a set of objectives that the psychology of learning suggests *can* be taught. After you have gone through this process, it is very unlikely that the set of objectives so derived would to any degree resemble some that you just happened to jot down.

Areas of Influence

What about those objectives that for some reason were not stated behaviorally? Perhaps they were learner and societal objectives for which there was little chance of attainment. Perhaps they were difficult to convert into operational language. Many teachers bristle at the thought that they have to write only behavioral statements and take responsibility for accomplishing every goal they have for their class. They point out that the art of teaching may be more advanced than the technology of measurement.

It is our position that the teacher should try to state goals operationally for all those that he is *seriously trying to accom-*

plish. However, it seems foolhardy to select objectives and evaluate teaching proficiency on the basis of very low probability ventures, such as promoting the pupil's "personality integration." One way to deal with this problem is to distinguish clearly between those goals for which you will accept *instructional responsibility* and those areas over which you would like to exert some influence, while recognizing that other factors, factors over which you have no control, are playing more important roles. Your operational instructional objectives should usually include some in the affective domain, but only for those attitudes and tendencies that are measurable and potentially modifiable in the classroom.

Summary

The product of Tyler's rationale is a set of objectives, behaviorally stated, derived from an inspection of data about the *learner, society*, and *subject matter*. These objectives have been checked for their value and consistency by the screen of *philosophy of education*, and for their potential attainment by the screen of *psychology of learning*. They have been inspected with regard to the behavior domain in which they fall and the level of the taxonomy that they reflect. Minimal standards of performance were added where possible.

Finally, a list of coordinate "areas of influence" may be prepared. These are broad goals for which the teacher does not accept complete instructional responsibility but that he does not intend to overlook.

A Note for the Future

The present trend is for curriculum specialists at the district and state levels to prepare exhaustive sets of behavioral objectives. Thus, the teacher's curricular job is somewhat simplified. He must merely *select* from the list those operational objectives he wishes to achieve. Ideally, test items designed to measure the attainment of the objectives would also be available; thus the teacher is not expected to function in the diverse roles of curriculum builder, instructional planner, and program evaluator. The teacher becomes, to a large extent, an objective *selector* rather than an objective *generator*. This procedure would seem very helpful, particularly with respect to hard-to-operationalize objectives. Thus, every teacher could presumably devote more time to the planning and evaluation of instruction, rather than to the admittedly arduous task of developing his own operationalized goals.

ADDITIONAL READING

Erikson, E. H., *Childhood and Society* (New York: W. W. Norton & Company, Inc., Publishers, 1950).

Goodlad, John I., *School Curriculum Reform in the United States* (Los Angeles: University of California Press, 1964).

Havighurst, R., *Human Development and Education* (New York: Longmans, Green & Company, Ltd., 1953).

Hill, Winfred F., *Learning: A Survey of Psychological Interpretations* (San Francisco: Chandler Publishing Company, 1963).

Phenix, Philip H. (ed.), *Philosophies of Education* (New York: John Wiley & Sons, Inc., 1961).

Piaget, Jean, and Barbel Inhelder, *The Early Growth of Logic in the Child, Classification and Seriation* (New York: Harper & Row, Publishers, 1964).

Soltis, Jonas F., *An Introduction to the Analysis of Educational Concepts* (Reading, Mass.: Addison-Wesley Publishing Co., Inc., 1968).

Steeves, Frank L., *The Subjects in the Curriculum—Selected Readings* (New York: The Odyssey Press, Inc., 1968).

Tyler, Ralph, *Basic Principles of Curriculum and Instruction* (Chicago: University of Chicago Press, 1950).

———, "New Dimensions in Curriculum Development," *Phi Delta Kappan*, XLVIII, No. 1 (September 1966).

5

An Instructional
Objective Analysis

In order to plan an effective instructional sequence a teacher must have two things: (1) a set of well-explicated operational objectives, and (2) a block of instructional time that needs to be filled. The teacher must, in some manner, order the objectives and place them in a suitable time frame, usually at least a semester in length and often a year. He must also face the even more difficult and important problem of breaking down a rather complex objective into simpler subobjectives and ordering these components in an optimal way.

The Sequencing Problem

The literature on sequence has for many years dealt with the sequence of *concepts* or *content* one wished to teach. Because *what the teacher did* was of overriding concern, the sequence question was more "What shall I present first?" rather than "What should be learned first?" Obviously, the two questions are intimately related, but the relationship has rarely been made explicit. Often the presentation of information by the

63

teacher has been interpreted as equal to the learning of information by students.

When instruction centered thus upon the teacher, sequence
problems were generally discussed only in terms of content.
Emphasis was on the "structure of the discipline." It was desirable, for example, to sequence content in one or more of
the following recommended ways: concrete-to-abstract, chronological, experientially familiar to experientially different, and
so on. Moreover, teachers were asked to prepare outlines on
content—"the scope and sequence" of a particular course.
Such a document typically referred to the concepts and generalizations of the subject-matter area and the order of their
appearance in the school year. Care was taken to encourage
the repetition of very important concepts as "strands" and
"threads" (or other sinewy metaphors) both within a particular
course and through a series of courses. Such careful planning
of subject matter should result in *logical* instructional plans;
however, the likelihood of their being effective with learners
is undetermined.

Certainly the subject-matter organization cannot be totally dis-
regarded. Certain mathematical concepts are prerequisite to
the learning of other mathematical concepts. Particular scientific principles are derived from the synthesis of simpler concepts. Or one specific order of subject matter may suggest
itself on a purely logical basis. Yet the difficulty of sequencing
does not subside in the presence of the subject-matter organization.

The requirement that we examine the *effect on students* of
exposure to a given content makes suspect many of the
above-mentioned sequencing orders, for instance concrete-to-
abstract. Yet in certain highly organized fields (like history,
where chronology is believed basic to the field) the sequence
of learner behavior designated may be made consonant with
the order of historical events. In other fields—for example
civics, English literature, or science—many traditional se-

quences that in the past had been highly accepted will require drastic modification, which may dramatically increase the chances that students will learn more efficiently. Instructional events will necessarily be described and ordered in content-plus-behavior modules. But even when the content-plus-behavior basis for planning classroom activities is accepted, there is still the substantial problem of determining *what* these components are and *how* they should be ordered. Precisely how should one go about planning instruction? How can the subobjectives be analyzed and ordered so that learning is promoted?

Gagné's Model

The teacher's first task is to identify the behaviors that will demonstrate the attainment of certain concepts. These behaviors will almost always depend on the successful mastery of one or more subobjectives. For example, a student cannot read a story unless he has learned the words in the vocabulary. A child cannot write his name unless he is able to form the individual letters that comprise it. A student cannot solve simultaneous equations until he can solve simple equations. How does one discover the appropriate subcomponents, that is, subobjectives, for a particular subject matter?

Gagné (1967) suggests that complex cognitive behaviors are invariably composed of simpler tasks, and that attainment of these tasks is necessary before the complex behavior can be demonstrated. Gagné has analyzed behavior into a hierarchy proceeding from the simplest kind of learning through the most complex. He hypothesizes that for learning any given task a structure exists. This structure includes the critical subtasks that a learner masters on his way to criterion performance. It is instructionally wise to attempt to identify subtasks for any instructional objective in order to avoid failures in mastery. Gagné (1965a) delineates separate levels for classifying tasks, that is, content-behavior goals. These levels are noted in order of increasing complexity. Gagné (1965b) implies that the order is hierarchical and that mastery at any elevated level assures mastery of all lower-level tasks, as illustrated below:

1. *Response differentiation.* Upon presentation of a stimulus definable within narrow physical limits, and no other stimulus, the learner makes a response that produces a copy of the stimulus, and no other response. For example, the learner would be able to repeat a pronounced word.

2. *Association.* Upon presentation of a stimulus, definable within narrow physical limits, and no other stimulus, the learner makes a response other than a copying response that identifies (names, codes) the stimulus and no other response. An example of this level might be for the student to say "California" when asked what is the most populous state.

3. *Multiple discrimination.* Upon presentation of two or more potentially confusable stimuli (physically defined), the learner makes an equal number of different responses that differentially identify these stimuli, and no other responses. A student might underline a triangle when instructed to do so, and not underline a rhomboid or circle.

4. *Behavior chains.* Upon presentation of a specific stimulus, the learner makes a series of two or more responses in a particular order, using no other order and no other responses. For example, a student could recite the "Pledge of Allegiance" when asked to do so.

5. *Class concepts.* Upon presentation of stimuli that differ widely in their physical appearance, the learner makes a response that identifies them as instances of a class and distinguishes them from instances belonging to other classes. For example, the student could indicate that "3/4" is a fraction numeral but that "5" is not.

6. *Principles*. Upon presentation of a situation containing stimuli classifiable as concept *a* and instruction to produce concept *b*, the learner performs the sequence a —— b. For example, the learner can apply a given rule (*a*) correctly in a new situation (*b*).

7. *Problem-solving strategies*. In discovering content principles applicable to a series of novel situations, the learner performs a mediating sequence *a′* —— *b′* in which *a′* is a class of concepts to be attended to selectively and *b′* is a class of responses intermediate to those required for completing the action. For instance, a student might be required to prove that an algebra statement is true by using previously learned rules.

Analysis of tasks based on such a scheme is obviously a complicated act; yet the underlying logic is not difficult. Gagné asserts that difficulties in learning may most often be attributed to overlooked prerequisites. One could inspect diagnostic data obtained from pupils to determine if they lack certain prerequisites. Careful post-tests could also be constructed to obtain data about pupil performance on subobjectives (en route objectives), information that could explain a major difficulty in teaching a given set of pupils. Yet the detailed preparation and categorization of subcomponents seems unduly demanding for the teacher who just wants to prepare efficient instruction and wishes to do so expediently.

The Taxonomic Approach

One alternative to traditional sequencing might be to attempt an oversimplification of behavior analysis by taking cues from Bloom's cognitive taxonomy. In much the same manner as in the use of Gagné's model, one could argue that attainment of knowledge-level tasks must precede higher types of cognitive objectives. The knowledge category encompasses at least three of Gagné's lower categories; thus classifications as minute or exact as in Gagné's model aren't necessary when using the cognitive taxonomy to guide one's sequence. However, basing the design of instruction solely on a knowledge-first strategy does not help much in ordering different behaviors within the knowledge category or within the higher levels. A second problem concerns the taxonomies themselves. Their essentially nonbehavioral character, compounded by the prose explanations of various levels, betrays some confusion and lack of distinctiveness between levels.

Another Approach

Lest one get too committed to or discouraged by the seemingly endless process of categorizing and classifying of tasks, we would like to offer a less esoteric suggestion. First, inspect the list of behavioral objectives to determine those that seem the most difficult in terms of the student responses called for. Most likely such objectives could be placed in the upper levels of either Bloom's or Gagné's system. Look at these "high-level" objectives to see what necessary subskills are included in them. The actual order of instruction is not so critical so long as all subtasks have been taught.

One way to approach the problem of task-component analysis is to look at each specific objective in terms of the following question: *"What does the learner need to be able to do before he can perform this task?"* While different analysts might derive different orders and even different components, it is likely that such an inspection will result in an instructional sequence that makes relatively few errors. Subsequent revisions in planning can improve the original analysis. For instance, suppose your objective were the following: "The learner will be able to spell aloud a given word when he is presented with the pronunciation of the word." A reasonable prerequisite task would be learning sound-to-letter correspondences. In addition, the learner would certainly need to identify letter names. To carry the analysis further, the learner would also need to be able to speak, and so on.

If the following task were your objective, what would be the necessary prerequisites?

> *Objective:* The learner will explain in an essay the conse-quences of adding a certain chemical to a mixture of other chemicals at stated heat and pressure levels.

Assuming this is not a rote task, and that the student did not simply recall the answer from a class lecture, he would have to be able to identify the properties of all chemicals involved in order to perform the task. He would also have to be able to state the effects of certain intensities of heat and pressure on the chemicals. He would also have to be able to describe cause-and-effect relationships to a certain degree. And again, he would have had to master basic communication skills, such as the ability to write or type in appropriate syntax.

It should be clear that many possible analyses would likely be generated for the same objectives were different people asked to do so, although the successive asking of the question "What does the learner have to be able to do?" may help exhaust the possibilities of component tasks. However, when there is no clear order implied, what is the appropriate course of ac-tion? Note the task analysis for the following objective:

> *Objective:* The learner will be able to write behavioral objec-tives in his subject area at the six levels of the cognitive taxonomy.

Even without becoming meticulous, one can see some of the varied routes open to the instructor of such a sequence. Does he teach about the taxonomy first (Path I) and then give in-struction in behaviorizing objectives (Path II)? Does he skip from path to path? How does he handle the whole area of subject-matter competence? (Certain skills, like the ability to

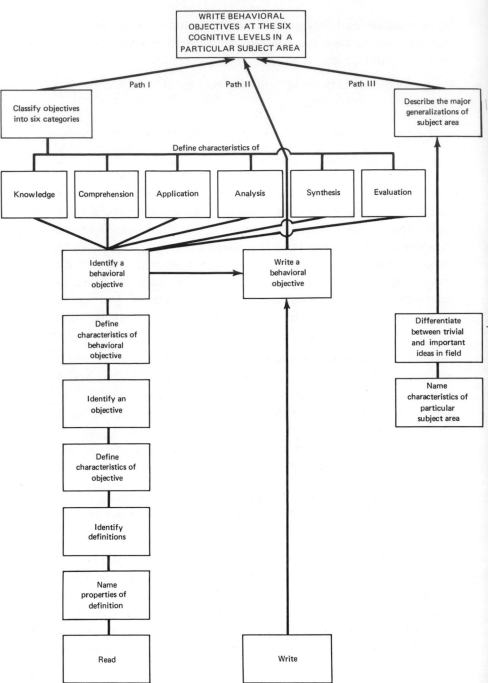

write English, have not even been included. When skills are obvious prerequisites, they may be treated as entry behaviors and presumed to be in the learner's repertoire. In most education courses subject-matter competence—Path III— is treated this way. Entry behaviors are assumed, sometimes unwisely, to exist.)

When the teacher is faced with multiple paths for a particular goal, he may have to consider the question of which path to deal with first in the light of other objectives planned for the class, so that prerequisites taught early and subsequently practiced extensively are those that are most important and most generalizable to other classroom objectives. Again, the teacher must determine the final answer to the sequence question empirically.

Asking "What does the learner need . . . ?" will enable the teacher to produce sequences of behavioral skills that will increase the likelihood of having a generally efficient instructional sequence the first time around. More important, the simplicity of applying such a strategy may leave him with sufficient energy to engage in the next stage of systematic instruction—teaching itself. The true measure of any instructional sequence is the experimental comparison of it against all other contending sequences. Such research, however, is rarely conducted, and almost never by a classroom teacher.

Summary

To sequence objectives, to analyze complex objectives into subobjectives, and to order these may be the hardest job of all when one considers what teaching is. The sequencing process is one the teacher must repeatedly inspect and probably revise in his attempt to improve his instruction. He will have to keep a few things in mind:

1. Analyze objectives into content-behavior modules, not just content.
2. Use guidance from a regularized scheme, such as that advocated by Gagné or Bloom.
3. To arrive at a first sequence, repeatedly ask the question, "What does the learner need to be able to do before he can perform this task?"
4. Clearly identify prerequisites not within your instructional responsibility.
5. Where possible, empirically verify sequences generated.

Pre-assessment

In order to decide if the objective he has selected for his class is appropriate, the teacher should use pre-assessment procedures. Pretesting is critical because it also helps establish what the class doesn't know—so that when, after instruction, the class demonstrates the desired competencies, the teacher can take the credit for promoting the desired changes.

Terminal Objectives

What should a pretest include? Ideally the teacher should pretest for all instructional objectives using items drawn from the same pool as the evaluation items. Too often teachers waste time teaching skills that, if they had pretested, they would have discovered the students already possessed. Thousands of suffering students have learned and relearned to exhaustion certain American history facts simply because teachers didn't pretest. The total number of pupil hours so misspent is staggering. A pretest, at the very minimum, should test the students' end-of-instruction skills. The information thus provided is simple: Do the students already possess the behavioral competencies to be taught?

En Route Objectives

A good pretest might also check the students' competence in regard to the en route objectives (subobjectives) to be treated. Perhaps a child can't sound out words, but can pronounce initial consonants. Such information would allow the teacher to spend time on skills other than initial sound practice. Discovering which students possess different en route skills also provides a basis for the teacher to individualize instruction or organize groups of students with similar competencies.

Entry Behaviors

Pretesting can serve another valuable function. The teacher can determine if the students have the skills necessary to have a chance for success in his instructional program. The teacher can discover if a student has mastered objectives he should have had in earlier courses. Probably the single most pervasive reason underlying instructional problems is the student's failure to master prerequisites that the teacher assumed he had already learned.

Formal or Informal Pretests?

Pretests, in which all students get the opportunity to respond to items measuring acquisition of terminal, en route, and prerequisite objectives, provide valuable information for the teacher; yet tests of such elaborateness aren't always necessary. In a beginning French class, a pretest that asked students to recite a sample dialogue would most likely be a waste of time. Perhaps a question such as, "How many of you can speak French?" would be more appropriate. When the probability is low that many of the students have much acquaintance with the content of the objectives, it is wise to limit the time taken in pretesting. Such pretesting can often be conducted by using a discussion format, a paper-and-pencil test, or an observation.

General Comments

When a teacher is pretesting, he should be sure to tell students beforehand that their test performance doesn't count toward their grades. Giving the students the correct answers to formal pretests is appropriate if a separate final test is used. If the same pretest is used as both a pretest and a post-test, giving correct answers has some obvious drawbacks.

Another pretesting consideration is whether the student will come to feel frustrated if he scores poorly on the test. This is a factor to consider, and may suggest that pretesting be conducted in small pieces rather than one overwhelming, course-covering session.

Pretesting is a necessary activity in systematic instruction. After pretesting, the teacher may have to adjust his objectives —adding some, discarding some, or modifying expected performance standards. After the teacher has made changes in the curricular part of the course—that is, the objectives—he can use the data generated from pretesting to help plan the instructional activities, for example, grouping.

Without pre-assessment, a teacher may run many risks. He may teach competencies already possessed by his learners, thus wasting much time that could have been spent on the acquisition of new, or more complex, abilities. The teacher could also err, if he has not pretested, by assuming prerequisite skills or entry behaviors not in his students' pre-instruction repertoires, and thus planning an instructional program too advanced for the students.

The (1) *analysis of the components of terminal objectives* in terms of what the learner has to be able to *do* before he can succeed at the task described by the objective, and (2) *pretesting* to measure the students' pre-instruction acquisition of the terminal, en route, and prerequisite behavior will set the stage for implementation of successful instruction.

ADDITIONAL READING

Gagné, R. W., *The Conditions of Learning* [New York: Holt, Rinehart & Winston, Inc., 1965(a)].

————, "Curriculum Research and the Promotion of Learning," *AERA Monograph Series on Curriculum Evaluation* (Chicago: Rand McNally & Company, 1967).

————, "The Analysis of Instructional Objectives for the Design of Instruction," in Robert Glaser, ed., *Teaching Machines and Programed Learning, II: Data and Directions* [Department of Audiovisual Instruction, National Education Association of the United States, 1965(b)].

6

Designing Instructional Activities

The third major component of our systematic instructional model requires that the teacher select activities for himself and his pupils that appear likely to promote the attainment of the objectives he has decided upon for the particular period of time involved, whether for a whole academic year or single class period. The initial step in this operation, as we indicated earlier, is a careful consideration of the kinds of preliminary—that is, entry and en route—behaviors the learner must master on his way to achieving the terminal behavior. The next step is setting up instructional activities that seem apt to work. In this chapter we shall examine several powerful instructional principles. By incorporating these principles in his plan of instruction, the teacher is more likely to bring about the desired terminal behaviors. However, as we shall indicate in a later chapter, the ultimate test of whether an instructional sequence works is exclusively a function of the learner's final attainment of goals. Accordingly, even with the use of these principles, the teacher must still verify the efficacy of instruction at its conclusion by attending to changes in the learners.

Revealing Objectives

Although it may sound almost theological to talk about a "revelation of objectives," the first principle to follow in setting up an instructional sequence is that the teacher should communicate to the learners the nature of the behavior changes he has in mind for them. There are several studies[1] suggesting that allowing learners to know what the teacher expects of them will enable them to achieve those intentions more efficiently. This result is only natural, for it is too often the case that learners spend much of their time trying to "out-psych" the teacher—that is, trying to guess what he will ask them on the final examination. By allowing the learner to know precisely what the objectives are, the teacher permits his pupils to focus their energies on relevant tasks and not waste their time on peripheral matters.

Objectives should be communicated to the learners in language that they will understand. If the teacher is dealing with very young children, for example, it is unlikely that he would communicate his objectives in the technical language that he might use to convey his goals to a colleague. Regardless of the simplicity of the language, there should be no doubt in the learner's mind about the instructor's intentions. It would be wrong, for example, to fall back into loose, nebulous language such as, "You will know how to work with simple arithmetic problems." Rather, the instructor should continue to use precise language that describes learner behavior; he may be obliged to give several examples to pupils in order to illustrate what he means. The time for communicating objectives should be early in an instructional sequence. It is not certain, how-

[1] G. V. Harrison, *The Instructional Value of Presenting Explicit Versus Vague Objectives* (California Educational Research Studies, 1967). R. R. Mager and J. McCann, *Learner-Controlled Instruction* (Palo Alto, Calif.: Varian Associates, 1961). R. M. Verhaegen, *The Effect of Learner-Controlled Instruction in a Tenth Grade Biology Curriculum* (unpublished M.A. thesis, University of California, Los Angeles, 1964).

ever, what capacity a particular group of learners may have for recalling objectives. For example, it does not seem reasonable with young pupils that a teacher should reveal objectives for a whole academic year at the beginning of the year, and then never again. Many objectives should probably be communicated on a monthly, weekly, or even daily basis. The important thing is that the learners understand precisely what is expected of them. They should know what the teacher wants them to do at the conclusion of instruction. They should know what to study for.

Some will raise an argument against revealing objectives to learners on the grounds that if students don't know exactly what will be involved in the evaluation of their behavior, they may study a wider range of material and, as a consequence, may learn much more than the teacher intended. The problem with this argument is that students often do "learn" more than the teacher intends but, generally, "learn" it only for a few days. That is, they study diligently for an examination, ranging widely over textbooks and lecture notes in order to amass all sorts of trivia for possible examination items. They carry this collection of minutiae stalwartly into an examination session, throw it back at the teacher, and then walk out of the class only to forget in a few days the vast majority of what they studied. The instructor who reveals objectives does run a risk of having the students study only what he considers important, to the exclusion of other things. This possibility is far less dangerous than the risks associated with the customary study of irrelevancies by a student who has no idea what the teacher will ask.

In some instances, particularly regarding affective objectives, it would be inappropriate to inform the learner of the instructor's objectives. For example, if a physical education teacher were planning to employ surreptitious techniques to observe the sportsmanship behavior that players displayed after losing a basketball game, he would obviously not tell the learners in advance; otherwise they might be on their guard and display (for the teacher's consumption) "jolly good sportsmanship" at every loss.

The teacher will find that by revealing objectives to the learners he creates a number of changes not only in their perceptions, but often in his own behavior as well. An example from our own experience is illustrative: In a class several years ago we had revealed course objectives to our learners, who paid careful attention to them. On one occasion, one of us elaborated on an entertaining but somewhat irrelevant anecdote. At its conclusion, a student from the class raised the following question: "Professor, will you please tell us to which of the course objectives your last fifteen minutes' worth of remarks were directed?" Such questions have a thoroughly intimidating effect upon the instructor, particularly when no reasonable answer is forthcoming. If both teacher and students are aware of course goals, the teacher will be more inclined to avoid irrelevancies.

The number of objectives that a teacher will develop for any course depends on the nature of the course. In some courses the teacher hopes for only a handful of comprehensive terminal behaviors at the close of the class. In others, there are myriad objectives. The number of objectives the teacher will wish to communicate to the students should be within the learners' ability to comprehend. Accordingly, the teacher will have to judge just how many objectives the students can assimilate in order to guide their studies.

Perceived Purpose

A principle strongly related to the act of revealing objectives is that of *perceived purpose*. According to this principle, the learner should be shown the value of what he is studying. In the first place, an effective description of *what* it is the learner is supposed to accomplish is most helpful. If, in addition, the learner can be shown *why* these objectives are worthwhile, it is far more likely that he will achieve the desired goals.

The principle falls in the general field of "motivation" that so many writers have described. More technically, the procedure of promoting perceived purpose is simply a scheme for establishing a "learning set" conducive to the pupil's attainment of objectives.

Many instructors assume that because they have selected particular objectives the students will automatically recognize that those goals are worthwhile. This is a delusion. Students often question the merits of the curriculum. They really can't see why they have to study much of the conglomerate material they encounter in each school day. Often their doubts are well founded; one would be hard put to explain any worth in much of what we include in our curricula. However, when there is some defensible reason for achieving a particular objective, this should be forcefully communicated to the learner. If the teacher searches for reasons to convince the learners that what they are studying is worthwhile and fails to find such reasons, it might be time for a reexamination of his instructional objectives.

There are several methods of communicating to the learners this "perception of purpose." The first method uses *deduction.* In this procedure the teacher actually spells out for the students why they should study the material. For example, if he thinks that the greatest appeal to a given group of learners would be created by showing them that they can use the subject matter in acquiring good post-high-school jobs or entrance into college, the teacher would explain this use, complete with illustrations.

In some instances the teacher has to decide among a number of possible purposes that the learner might find reasonable for a given set of objectives. Sometimes, it is likely that the most worthwhile reason for accomplishing the objective is not as enticing to learners as a secondary purpose might be. We might all, for example, wish students to pursue our subject matter for the love of learning, but frequently student motives will be more utilitarian, and we may be obliged to appeal to such motives.

A second procedure for promoting perceived purpose is *induction*. In using this technique, the teacher allows the students to generate their own reasons for learning the objectives, possibly as a consequence of carefully staged activities by the teacher. The teacher might, for instance, suggest a series of ideas to the learners that will make it very probable that they will, on their own, perceive the value of certain objectives. The teacher might even ask the students to suggest their own reasons for studying a subject matter. Or he might describe a very dramatic event and ask them to consider the relevance of this event to their own lives. For example, if a current labor-management dispute in the state had caused a number of parents to be temporarily laid off from work, reference to the dispute might stimulate the students' study of a related unit in a government class.

One might also argue that the teacher who employs the threat of poor grades and notes to parents, or the promise of good grades and free time—that is, the teacher who uses *extrinsic rewards*—is employing an effective motivation device. The teacher might also be considered to be motivating the class if he uses *exhortation* by simply asking the students to "study hard." Although in many instances the use of extrinsic rewards and exhortation may help to motivate a class, it is more consistent with the general theme of this principle to attempt to provide the learners with insight regarding the *purpose* of the instructional objectives.

Appropriate Practice

Of the many principles from the field of instructional psychology that a teacher can utilize, perhaps the most potent is that of *appropriate practice*. According to this principle, the teacher must provide opportunities during an instructional sequence for the learner to behave in a fashion consistent with the instructional objectives. To put it more simply, the teacher must let the students practice what they will be called upon to do in displaying mastery of the instructional objectives. As we shall describe later, there are several forms of this principle; regardless of the particular form, a number of research investigations attest to the instructional power of practice. Common sense alone would tend to corroborate the utility of the principle. When we want people to engage in a particular kind of behavior, like shooting a basketball or reading a poem, it is reasonable that the best way to have them eventually become skilled is to give them practice in performing the skill. Other things being equal, the more appropriate practice activities a teacher can build into an instructional sequence, the more likely the learner will be to achieve the objectives.

Equivalent Practice

One type of appropriate practice the teacher might provide for the students is practice of behavior that is exactly like the terminal behavior described in the objective. Such activities are designated *equivalent practice*. This means that the instructional stimuli will be identical to those used, for example, on the final examination. In addition, the learner's expected responses will be identical to those called for during the evaluation. For instance, if a student is to respond orally to written test exercises, equivalent practice would demand that he be given a chance to make oral responses to written exercises of the same kind as those used in the test.

There are many instances in which the teacher cannot have the students engage in *exactly* the same behavior because they would thereby become familiar with the particular test questions to be used. Instead, the use of equivalent practice implies that the teacher can draw questions from the general category of those that might be asked of the learner in evaluations. For example, perhaps the teacher wants a student to generate satisfactory responses to hypothetical problem situations that he constructs. It would be necessary to construct problem situations similar to those that he will be asked to face on the final examination. The teacher clearly would not want to give him the very same items during practice sessions.

It is not completely clear how much equivalent practice should be provided for the learners. In general, it is probably wiser to err in the direction of too much rather than too little. The distressing truth is that few teachers provide *any* equivalent practice for their learners. Very frequently teachers give students a totally new kind of intellectual exercise on the final examination, thinking that this really tests the students' understanding of the subject matter. Often the behavior called for on this final test is extremely worthwhile; but the students should be given a chance to practice that behavior in order to find out whether they are progressing satisfactorily *prior* to the time that they are finally tested. Equivalent practice should be provided for en route objectives as well as terminal objectives.

Analogous Practice

A second form of appropriate practice provides that the student be given an opportunity to practice behavior that is similar, but not identical, to the terminal behavior. In this practice situation, called *analogous practice*, there may be modifications in the nature of the instructional stimuli or in the nature of the learner's response. He may be required to perform the same intellectual operations but respond in a somewhat different way. For instance, instead of answering multiple-choice questions, he might be asked to make responses about the correctness of a series of choices presented one at a time. Or he might be asked to respond orally, when the actual evaluation calls for written responses. In the same vein, there might be subtle modifications in the presentation stimuli. There are also analogous practice situations in which slight changes are made in both the instructional stimuli and the learner's response. There is a particularly strong argument for analogous practice opportunities on the grounds that they permit the teacher to provide more *variety* for the students than would otherwise be the case.

Not just any activities for learners that concern the topic being taught should be considered analogous practice. Ideally, if the instructional objective calls for selected responses, the learner should be required, at least intellectually, to make selections. If the objective calls for constructed responses, the learner should be required, at least intellectually, to construct.

We do not mean to suggest here that equivalent practice is intrinsically superior to analogous practice. There are some instances in which the same level of student proficiency can undoubtedly be promoted through the use of analogous *or* equivalent practice. However, the use of some kind of appropriate practice during an instructional sequence would seem to be such a powerful instructional method that all teachers are urged to employ it.

Knowledge of Results

Closely related to the principle of appropriate practice is the principle of *knowledge of results*. According to this principle, provisions should be made to enable the learner to determine the adequacy of his responses shortly after he makes them. For practical purposes it is recommended that knowledge of results be provided for the learner at least within one hour after he makes his responses, but preferably results should be available immediately. The one-hour limitation is set down only to encourage the teacher to provide for knowledge of results within the same class period in which the learner's responses occurred.

How can knowledge of results be provided? There are many ways in which the teacher can allow the student to find out whether his responses are correct or incorrect. The teacher can, for example, post a series of questions and correct answers shortly after the students make their responses. Students can exchange papers among each other for marking. Students can check their own papers while the teacher reads the correct answers. The important thing here is for the teacher to give the students some way of finding out whether their responses are on target.

Much evidence in the research literature supports the idea that there is a positive learning dividend to be derived from allowing students to know whether their responses are correct or incorrect. In order for the teacher to adhere scrupulously to this rule in the case of homework assignments, it may be necessary to send the correct answers home with the students so that they can tell if their responses were right. It may take some time to promote the practice in some students to first make their responses, *then* check the right answers. Such homework practice should ordinarily not be counted toward the student's course grade.

In certain cases it is very difficult to provide knowledge of results because the student is essentially generating a *constructed* rather than a *selected* response. In the case of selected responses, such as in choosing the correct answers from multiple-choice questions, it is relatively simple to give knowledge of results. In the case of constructed responses where the learner must generate a new response, it is sometimes exceedingly difficult to anticipate how the learner will respond and, therefore, to indicate immediately whether he is correct or incorrect. One scheme for providing knowledge of results under these conditions is to allow the student to respond, then to have the teacher describe the criteria upon which the response will be judged. Having done so, he may provide a few illustrations of correct and incorrect answers. The student is then permitted to assess the probable adequacy of his own response on the basis of these criteria and illustrations. While there are some problems regarding the learner's certainty under a scheme such as this, the attempt is considerably better than nothing.

Differentiated Instruction

Another principle of great utility in planning instructional sequences is to differentiate instruction for the learners. There are at least two methods of differentiating instruction. One of these is to modify the objectives for different students so that particular learners are given different objectives. For example, those with extremely high ability could receive additional or more challenging objectives, while those with less ability would receive fewer or less challenging objectives. A second scheme for differentiating instruction involves the use of different *means* to accomplish identical instructional *ends*. In the present discussion we are concerned primarily with the latter type of differentiation, although the former technique has obvious advantages.

When differentiating means of instruction, the teacher should choose instructional procedures that appear to be consonant with the abilities, interests, and prior achievements of given learners. Unfortunately there is not much evidence to indicate what these procedures would be, but at this point it seems reasonable that the teacher might move in a more gradual sequence of en route activities in the case of less able youngsters. With the gifted student, the teacher could modify his teaching in some way so that it capitalizes on the learner's interest and ability. Differentiation is far more easily preached than practiced. Surely, effective differentiation means more than giving additional practice opportunities to the students who are having difficulty. If students differ in their ability to recognize the value of education, differentiation would require that far more time be spent with some students than with others in establishing perceived purpose.

The Attainment of Affective Objectives

Most of the foregoing remarks in this chapter have been directed to the attainment of cognitive objectives. There are instances in which some of the principles suggested here would not apply with respect to the accomplishment of affective objectives. For instance, the principle of appropriate practice does not seem to make much sense when the teacher promotes, as an affective consequence, high scores on a particular kind of attitudinal measuring device. The teacher would not ordinarily want to give the attitudinal measuring device to the learner in advance of evaluation in order to give him practice in obtaining high scores on it.

Relatively few guides exist for the attainment of affective objectives. Generally speaking, if the teacher wishes to promote more positive learner response toward the subject matter, it certainly makes sense to have as many positive factors associated with the subject matter as possible. This approach, generally based on a "contiguity" theory of learning, would suggest that the teacher do as much as possible to make the whole learning atmosphere warm, supportive, satisfying, and so on. Until some time in the future when more definitive principles will have been developed for designing instructional sequences to accomplish affective objectives, we shall have to do some question-begging regarding these techniques, because, as we mentioned earlier, there are differences in procedures used for the attainment of affective, cognitive, and psychomotor objectives.

Even though current knowledge is limited regarding the attainment of affective objectives, you should not underestimate the power of the systematic instructional model recommended here for the achievement of those goals. For example, if the teacher goes to the trouble of clearly delineating behavioral indices that he thinks reflect important affective outcomes, then discovers that he is not achieving them, at least he can do some modifying in his instructional sequence with the expectation of achieving the desired outcomes in the future. We would recommend that teachers try using a "table of random learning activities" in designing their instructional sequences, but be willing to assess the merits of those selections continually in terms of learner behavior at the conclusion of instruction, changing the sequence if necessary.

ADDITIONAL READING

Glaser, Robert, ed., *Teaching Machines and Programed Learning, II: Data and Directions* (Department of Audiovisual Instruction, National Education Association of the United States, 1965).

————, "Ten Untenable Assumptions of College Instruction," *Educational Record* (Spring 1968).

Lumsdaine, A. A., "Instruments and Media of Instruction," in N. L. Gage, ed., *Handbook of Research on Teaching* (Chicago: Rand McNally & Company, 1963).

Wallen, Norman E., and Robert M. W. Travers, "Analysis and Investigation of Teaching Methods," in N. L. Gage, ed., *Handbook of Research on Teaching* (Chicago: Rand McNally & Company, 1963).

7

Classroom Transactions

The ideas concerning derivation of curricular objectives, careful analysis of their sequence, pre-assessment, and knowledge of useful instructional principles combine to give a teacher the opportunity to make an impact on the learning of his pupils. But while these elements are considered essential to the act of systematic instruction, they are not sufficient. Understanding these principles, even possessing the ability to apply them, does *not* equal the act of teaching. In some cohesive, coherent way, the use of principles of learning has to be integrated into the situation the teacher is in, related to the kind of person he is, and cast into a form the teacher can cope with. In this present discussion we shall deal with ways that teachers can organize classroom activities and present or monitor instruction.

The Lecture

The teacher usually accomplishes his goals by employing verbal behavior. How can this talk be organized best to help students learn? Among the modes of behavior a teacher could select is that of lecturing. Any identifiable segment of information presented orally might be titled a lecture, be it a 45-minute formal presentation or a five-minute talk. A lecture is neither good nor bad in itself; it must be evaluated in the context of the objective to which it seeks to contribute. Obvious as this statement may sound, there are many teachers and supervisors who viscerally recoil from the process of lecturing. They may justify their derision in one fashion or other: "A lecture is inappropriate for the age level, inappropriate for the topic, and so forth."

While lectures certainly do have identifiable limitations, for example, failing to provide many opportunities for students to practice relevant behavior (other than note-taking), the lecture still can be used profitably with learners of almost any age level. The primary purpose of a lecture is the presentation of ideas. Other forms of presentation—the duplicated page, for example—might serve adequately in many instances. Still, a quality that is disturbingly ineffable pervades a good lecture. It is centered on the lecturer's ability to communicate his feeling about the topic. He does this in his manner of delivery, his intonation patterns, his emphases, his gesticulations. He can turn a mediocre subject into a compelling one, or an intriguing topic into a nap.

To be a good lecturer, one needs practice and feedback. With practice, a lecturer loses his academic snootiness and delivers something less exalted but just as effective. A lecturer also needs to know whether he does what he is doing well. He should attempt to determine if his rate of speech is right, if he uses vocabulary appropriate to his students, and if he speaks loudly enough. The overall effectiveness of the teacher in this regard can be grossly inferred from the pupil performance measures used to evaluate his teaching; but some method for obtaining more exact information, either student- or colleague-generated, should be designed.

Most of the following "wisdom" is nonempirical in derivation. It reflects some of the current lore of professors of speech.

It has to do with the attributes of semiformal communication. We present it only in the event that you do not have much experience talking in front of people (students are people) and in case you need some broad cues to guide you.

Planning the lecture

What should you do when you decide that the most efficient way to present material relevant to a given objective is to lecture? You must, first of all, limit the amount of time you will lecture so that it is appropriate to the learners' age. Even in the best situations, half-hour lectures broach the limit at any age level. Next, it is important to plan what you are going to say. You may prepare at the level of specificity that satisfies you, but there is a danger of overly meticulous planning. Some teachers who specialize in reading their lecture notes verbatim also seem to be those who are the most boring. Completely written lectures offer false security, because if you lose your place it may be very difficult to find it, which can be somewhat disconcerting to you and to your class. Probably the best method is to prepare lecture notes in outline form, listing words or phrases that trigger associations for you. You must remember that lecturing ability is sharpened with experience, and that you will probably improve over time. But planning *what* you are going to say will prevent your rambling on without positive reasons for doing so.

In planning your lecture, remember to devise questions to ask your students. Questions posed directly to your students can help you gauge how well the class is learning. Rhetorical questions can also be used to help stimulate the students' involvement. You might initiate the lecture with a series of questions for the students to think about and, perhaps, to answer at the conclusion of your talk. Another technique to aid student involvement is the use of examples in your lecture. If you can draw parallels to experiences that your students might have had, it is more probable that your lectures will get through.

If the illustrations you choose are humorous, that's even better, so long as they are illustrations of important points you intend to make. The worst use of humor is the joke-book story told to "kick off" a talk. These jokes seem to function as swill to the conscience: once the ritual is out of the way, the lecturer can forget about trying to interest his listeners. Inadvertent misuses of humor are particularly frequent when one is teaching adolescents. Secondary-school-age students are often the hardest critics. If you try to be funny with them by using standard, musty jokes, you're likely to fail. Such failure can tag you as the prototype anathema of all teenagers—"square," "corny," or whatever the current "out" epithet happens to be. Once attached, it's a hard label to shed. So if you do use humor, have it appear to be spontaneous rather than beside the point.

Another important rule in lecturing is always to summarize the points you've made in the lecture. Summaries underscore the information to be emphasized for the student, who may be so carried away with your eloquence that he focuses on minor considerations. Instead of your dutiful recitation of the summary, you could ask different students to summarize orally what you've said; or you might allocate a few minutes at the conclusion of the lecture for the students to write summaries and then call on a number of students to read them.

Delivery

The delivery of a lecture ought to be a casual rather than a harrowing encounter for both you and the students. Highly oratorical, bombastic styles tend to embarrass listeners and are usually not very effective. A good lecturer will try to employ conversational style, using enthusiasm (if he's up to it). Lectures have to be fairly loud, usually louder than you expect. Many teachers talk to their classes too meekly to be heard, and hosts of discipline problems are thereby spawned. Student teachers also often speak much too rapidly to be understood.

This rapid speech can be a sign of nervousness and may really be frustrating for students who are not proficient slur-decipherers. Fast rates of speech can be particularly detrimental in classrooms where standard English is not the native language spoken at home.

Another pitfall for newer teachers is their tendency to use esoteric language. This is often done to demonstrate how bright, well-educated, and generally important they feel. Young instructors teaching in secondary schools may use inflated language as a way to help them feel older and more suited to their role. However, the use of vocabulary beyond the students' (or teacher's) level of comprehension would seem to have generally negative consequences.

Even when the teacher isn't consciously trying to employ elevated semantics, he may be speaking in words that are not well understood by the students. This practice is easy to account for when one considers the pervasively rarified atmosphere of college from which a teacher emerges. He may take for granted that he is communicating with his students but may still be missing most of them. If a teacher uses new words, he should define them in the lecture itself. He might also ask students to explain a word for the rest of the class if he suspects some students do not understand.

It is also helpful to use simple sentences that tend to be short rather than long. A complicated sentence may be fine in print, but almost unintelligible when it is spoken. A listener can devote too much attention to waiting for the verb in a convoluted sentence and miss a relatively important point.

Another technique of presentation that a teacher might attend to in his lecturing is physical movement during the course of a lecture. Many teachers seem to be on an invisible five-foot leash attached to their desk. They never stray into areas where the students are. Lecturers should move freely in the class. They can thereby stimulate a little more interest (moving targets, and the like). They can also better see what is happening with the students.

Another rather obvious "speech-course" suggestion is to try to look at the faces of the students, engaging in the time-honored art of "eye contact." Students feel a bit more interested when they can observe their teacher paying close attention to them. You might also try, as you lecture, to determine if you are engaging in any speech habits that might disturb your students. Favorite among many are: "uh," "you know," and "okay" interpolated at frequent intervals. Uses of such fillers are usually nervous reactions and reflect an oral attempt to buy time for the lecturer's thought processes; obviously their overuse can be deadly. Monotones instead of usual intonation patterns can also detract from worthwhile ideas. The lecturer may engage in unnerving physical habits without being aware of them. He may tug on his ear, flap his hands around, blink, pace in a regular pattern, or clear his throat, all to the distraction of his class. These behaviors and many of the others previously discussed are often unnoticed by the offender. For that reason, the opportunity to videotape his teaching can allow the teacher to pick up many different cues from viewing the playback. Although it can be a trifle shocking to his ego, it is an extremely worthwhile experience. If videotape equipment is not readily available to you, a good substitute might be to have a colleague watch you teach and observe presentation flaws.

Remember, all of the above reflect general feelings of people who observe lecturers. In reality a teacher could stand rigidly still, speak at an hysterical rate in a monotonic screech, punctuate alternate sentences with "okay" or with terrible jokes, use language of a highly technical nature, and still produce desired results with students; but such seems unlikely.

Discussion

Another popular form in which instruction is often set is the discussion. There is something delightfully democratic about discussions. They aren't as teacher-directed as lectures, and, presumably, they allow the students a chance to develop their own ideas. Activities described as discussion can range in structure from rigid question-and-answer periods to group encounters that appear more psychotherapeutic than instructional.

Discussion procedures are so esteemed that complete schools of instruction are based on them. For a prominent example, nondirective teaching—where the teacher shifts complete instructional responsibility to the students—depends solely on the discussion for its transactions. Described by Nathaniel Cantor in *The Dynamics of Learning* (1946), among other writings, nondirective teaching removes the teacher from his usual role as information dispenser, confirmation provider, and limit setter. The nondirective teacher's position is more akin to a group leader who is reluctant to lead. Success with this approach has been found with mature students in advanced topics.

One of the difficulties in nondirective teaching and in the use of discussion in general lies in choosing the kind of topic that can be discussed. If the topic demands evaluation, if it is a question of interpretation or choice, discussion may be a reasonable medium through which the objective can be achieved. Discussion can, in a sense, function as analogous practice for certain objectives—for example, writing an essay in which the student defends a value position.

Discussion also has great utility in bringing about concrete affective changes in learners. Such alterations in attitudes or values are extremely difficult to achieve when the learner is not given a chance to make his feelings known. Skilled use of the discussion model permits the shaping of attitudes in a social context.

Basic, then, to the selection of discussion as a classroom technique is a consideration of what the desired outcomes of such an activity are. If the behavior to be changed is at the knowledge level of Bloom's cognitive taxonomy, discussion is likely to be an inefficient method to employ. If the objective is at the evaluation level of the cognitive taxonomy or in the affective domain, it would seem much more likely that discussion would be used sometime in the instructional sequence. Discussion is typically time-consuming, and topics selected for discussion should therefore be important enough to warrant such time investments.

**Planning for
a discussion**

Once discussion is selected to aid in the achievement of important objectives, and thus the time to be spent somewhat justified, how does one go about it? A major mistake novice teachers make is assuming that "discussion" can take care of itself. For most teachers, this is not so. Student teachers are sometimes put into difficult positions when discussions listed in lesson plans fail to materialize and they are left with an empty twenty minutes in the lesson. When a teacher *plans* the discussion, at least in its grossest structure, such unnerving events are less likely to occur. First he must select a topic on which the students have sufficient background. If he expects the learner to operate on the analysis or evaluation level of the taxonomy, the learner must at least have mastered the knowledge level. How unfortunate is the teacher who decides to discuss a relatively entrancing topic—such as "Should inflation be left unchecked?"—and finds that the students haven't the faintest idea of what economy, inflation, or balloons are. The insistence that learners possess desired entry competencies militates against the use of spontaneous discussions. Planning for discussions also must take account of the teacher's level of discussion-leading competence. He should be rather thoroughly versed in the topic and, moreover, have considered the relevance of the discussion to other instructional tactics he wishes to employ in order to have learners achieve criterion performance.

A set of questions and anticipated answers can offer a convenient guide for conducting the discussion. The teacher must also be rather deliberate in the use of perceived purpose or other motivating techniques. Ideally, the topic itself should be provocative and interest-arresting. If the students fail to see why the topic is important to them, their hostility can increase in direct relationship to the length of the classroom time allocated to the discussion.

Conducting a discussion

Even with all of the above considerations duly accounted for, discussions are not a cinch. Pupils may need much assistance in the process of discussion. For example, students may have considerable difficulty in responding to each other directly without intervening clarification or approbation on the part of the teacher. Students may, at the outset, be generally unwilling to take risk positions in a discussion, preferring the safety of the text's (or teacher's) dogma. Simple procedural decisions, such as whether hands should be raised, to whom comments should be directed, how loud the remarks should be, can be established via expectations stated by the teacher before any real discussion develops. Simple signals, such as rearranging the chairs in a circle, can help establish the free atmosphere generally thought to be desirable for discussions.

Initial ventures into discussion ought to be kept short, especially before the procedures are mastered by the students. Fifteen minutes is the outside limit (a totally arbitrary statement—it could as easily be fourteen or seventeen minutes) for secondary school classes without previous experience in discussion. Even when the class is quite skilled in discussion, thirty minutes can usually satiate the teacher's and students' desires.

A teacher may be placed in difficult positions during a typical discussion, primarily because of his conflicting instructional goals. Generally, a teacher desires to keep the discussion centered about a limited problem. He can do the best when he does not follow up on student comments that are tangential or irrelevant to the topic. Yet the teacher usually wishes to encourage freedom of discourse for his students. It is a tricky managerial task to obtain the right mix, but hopefully it can be accomplished over time. This may mean that on occasion the teacher must suggest that highly interesting sidelights mentioned by students be deferred to a later time.

Teachers who use discussion often suggest that all students be responsible contributors. This goal seems healthy, but generally unrealistic. Certainly discussion ought not to be the bore it often is when the teacher and one or two students engage in a dialogue that interests only them. However, certain teachers assume that an open grade book, and a mark for each contributor, is a fine way to deal with the problem of maximizing responses. A more reasonable approach might be calling on specific students to contribute. Many teachers suggest preparing students so that they always know they are responsible for something written based on a discussion. Such a procedure supposedly reduces the number of students who would otherwise tune out on nonteacher comments. If the discussion is placed in an appropriate practice context, the teacher can reasonably expect responses from most students.

Whether student-generated or not, discussions should always be summarized by someone. Presumably this summary fixes the major outcomes in students' minds and provides a finishing touch to a procedure in which all relevant comments and conclusions may not be remembered by some.

Demonstrations

Both lecture and discussion need augmentation. Teachers often employ demonstration in the classroom to serve this purpose. In performance classes such as physical education, art, and industrial arts, demonstration is basic to much of the instruction. It is also used, to a lesser extent, in other areas whenever the teacher resorts to a real or schematic representation of relationships through use of the chalkboard. Obviously there are times when illustration through demonstration is much more efficient than verbal description.

The guidelines for conducting demonstrations are fairly simple. First, be sure you can do what you are supposed to demonstrate. Chemistry teachers are often described as great demonstration planners but sloppy executioners. "If the experiment had worked we would have seen . . . " can be their slogan, and the anticlimax of it all must contribute to the students' negative affect toward the instructional topic. Demonstrations fail because of poor planning. Extension cords, plug adapters, and audiovisual equipment are the nemeses of demonstrations. Plan the demonstration so that everyone can see it. This may mean that you have to move students or chairs to accommodate everyone adequately, or you may have to give replays for smaller groups of students. Also take care that visual stimuli— printing on the chalkboard or on charts—are large enough to be seen easily. Be sure that appropriate safety precautions are taken. Also try to plan your demonstrations to precede a practice session. Demonstrations, because they are sometimes breaks in instructional routine, may be offered up by the teacher as rewards for the successful culmination of instruction. More properly, a demonstration serves as a model for some task subsequently expected of the students.

During the demonstration it may be useful to ask specific questions of the students to be sure that they understand what is happening. "Do you all understand?" is not an appropriate question. Also, if you are demonstrating a procedure of some sort, be certain to give thorough instruction in a single method before introducing shortcuts or other variations. In most instances, teachers should be happy if the student can perform the task at all.

A teacher may become so enamored of giving demonstrations (they usually are fun; the spotlight is on the teacher's proficiency) that he may do them very frequently. There is nothing wrong with demonstrations as such, but they tend to reduce activity in the students and perhaps reduce the probability that the students learn effectively. Before engaging in a complex demonstration, a teacher should ask himself whether a legitimate instructional need will be served. As with the use of discussion, it may be a good idea to ask the students to do some sort of post-demonstration write-up or statement to promote their attention and responsiveness.

Questions

Another common classroom occurrence is the questioning activity of teachers. Teachers enjoy the prerogative of asking questions and assuming that they'll be answered. Throughout lecturing, demonstration, and certainly discussion, questions can provide the teacher with a procedure to stimulate the students' thinking. The teacher can also use the answers given by students to check the en route efficacy of his instructional efforts. Questions, of course, may be oral or written, and so may their answers. Written questions and answers seem more formal but generally reflect closer approximations of equivalent practice than do rapid-fire oral questions and answers. In any case, the questions should be planned in a meaningful order. A question asked out of sequence can invalidate a series of other good questions. It can also be much too difficult for the students to answer without the base of other properly ordered questions and answers. In programed instruction, such a procedure is called sequence prompting; that is, previously elicited responses help the learner to make the correct response to a particular question.

Questions that can be answered by "yes" and "no" should generally be avoided. Help (Sanders, 1966) has been provided in planning questions that illustrate the different levels of Bloom's taxonomy of the cognitive domain. One might imagine that many questions answerable by "yes" or "no" reflect behavior at the knowledge level. Hypothetical situations, "What would happen if . . . ?" or conditional questions, "How would . . . ?" or "How could . . . ?" necessarily involve responses at higher than the lowest level in the taxonomy.

Questions can also serve an "organizing" function. A general question asked prior to a lecture or demonstration might enable a student to concentrate his attention on the most relevant aspects of the instruction. In determining the format for questions, it is generally best for the teacher to be guided by his objectives. If an objective calls for a selected response, the question in class should allow the students to practice that form of responding.

Certain techniques may be employed during oral question-and-answer periods that should make the session more productive. For one, always ask the question first, then call on the student, rather than the reverse. If you say "Howard, how would you . . . ?" every non-Howard in the class may stop attending to what you are saying. It is certainly better to say "How would you . . . , Howard?" because such phrasing increases the chance that more students will attend to the question. To be of most use, the teacher should couple this procedure with a general restraint in repeating questions once he has asked them clearly. Some students have been conditioned to ignore classroom activities until they hear their name called. Then they can ask for a repetition of the question and still be in moderately good shape. The teacher's refusal to precue questions with a particular student's name and restraint in repeating clearly asked questions can generally improve the level of attention he will obtain from the class.

In dealing with pupil responses, a teacher can also follow some methodological hints to improve the outcomes of questioning periods. It is a good idea to avoid repeating what the student has answered:

Teacher: What is the capital of Mexico, Sally?
Sally: Mexico City.
Teacher: Mexico City.

This unexciting verbal interchange does much more than just bore; it tends to reinforce the idea that no classroom response is legitimate until it has the approval (by reiteration) of the teacher. Aside from the obviously poor psychological consequences such behavior has, it results in the class's general inattention to remarks made by anyone other than the teacher. For one thing, meaningful discussion sessions are less likely with such teacher behavior. The teacher should encourage students to answer loudly and refrain from repeating the student response unless it is truly noteworthy or the student is a special case (one who seems to need a lot of support, for example).

When a student answers incorrectly, the teacher probably should (in the name of knowledge of results) indicate that this is so. However, he will have to be tactful if he wants students to continue to answer his questions freely. Similarly, answers that are ungrammatical or that reflect poor usage of the language may be corrected even if the substance of the answer is adequate. However, it is important to consider the kind of student, gregarious or reticent, who is making the response, and the general nature of his language, standard or dialect. Essentially, the teacher must decide on the nature of his objectives, whether he is assessing the substance or form or an amalgamation of the two in the student's response. If the right answer is more important than the right language, the teacher should correct grammatical errors only in severe cases, where communication is hampered. Properly planned and implemented questions can be the source of much of the pleasure one derives from teaching.

Other Activities

Besides lecture, demonstration, discussion, and questions, the teacher and students engage in many other activities together. The procedural ones—for example, roll-taking and clerical work—are the bane of most teachers. If clerical assistance is not available, a teacher might consider using students to help him, if they are old enough. Keeping track of excuses, homework, library passes, and so on can usually be delegated to a student. Intellectually less able youngsters can feel rather special when given procedural responsibilities of this order. It may be best to establish a general classroom routine, a particular time when students know homework is to be passed in and so on.

During instruction students also complete homework, read in texts, read aloud, solve problems, paint, go to the chalkboard, and engage in 74 other activities. How does the teacher plan for all of this to occur and keep in mind the instructional principles which are supposed to increase his pupils' performance? The way most teachers have coped with this problem is through the lesson plan.

Lesson plans

It is usual for courses in instructional methods to make a big issue of the lesson plan. It is important. It is the teacher's rational anticipation of what will occur in the classroom, before the serendipity of working with people warps it. It can serve as a guide and a constraint. But most of all (and this seems to be what so many prospective teachers overlook), the teacher must be comfortable with his lesson plan. Lest this sound like a fetish, comfort here means that (1) the lesson plan is written at a level of generality upon which the teacher can function; (2) the plan is not a finished document designed for publication, but is a quickly prepared outline from which the teacher can work. Too many times teachers, especially student teachers, prepare beautifully worded lesson plans, then either leave the teaching profession because "it is too much work" or abandon the idea of lesson plans altogether because they can't imagine such perpetual drudgery. Usually, either course of action is unfortunate. Hence, the time we devote here to lesson planning is brief.

Lesson plans need have only four major ingredients to function adequately.

1. The *objective*, behaviorally stated.
2. *Materials*, if any unique to the lesson (do not list chalk, erasers, and the like).
3. A description of *pupil* and *teacher activities* with estimated time devoted to them.
4. *Homework* assignments, if any.

The teacher-pupil description provides the most trouble for teachers.

A lesson plan could look like this:

Objective: To have students acquire ability to solve selected perimeter problems

Materials: Rulers

Activities:

Time	Teacher	Students
8:25–8:30	*Roll, etc.*	
8:30–8:45	*Tell class objective; explain perimeter demonstration at board. Ask questions. Summarize procedure.*	
8:45–9:05	*Assist.*	*In pp. 49–51, work problems 1, 3, 4, 7*
9:05–9:15	*Discuss problems if students have errors.*	*Put problems on board.*
9:15–9:30	*Homework assignment.*	*Pp. 49–51, problems 2, 5, 6, 8, 9, 10*

Such a lesson plan provides sufficient guidance for a teacher who feels fairly secure in the topic of perimeters. It provides some helpful organizational cues, too. First, the teacher has an estimate of how long different activities should take. He knows that he must stop preliminary explanations by 8:45, that in-class work starts by 9:05, and that he must begin to give the homework assignments by 9:15. Use of real-time referents, rather than "five minutes for homework assignment," makes the teacher's job during instruction easier, he doesn't have to continually subtract elapsed time from the class period. On the other hand, if the teacher is going to use a lesson plan in two classes with different time limits, the general-time approach is better.

Some semicompulsive student teachers have turned in lesson plans whose activity sections look more like this:

Activities:

	Teacher	Students
8:25–8:30	Call roll.	Answer if present.
8:30–8:45	"The objective for today is to be able to solve perimeter problems." See lecture notes.	Listen.
8:45–9:05	Walk around helping those in need.	Work perimeter problems on pp. 49–51, solving problems 1, 3, 4, 7.

Great detail is fine if the teacher can manage it, but lesson plans should generally be written lean. They should function as a guide. Particular suggestions for preparing lesson plans in addition to the stating of objective, materials, activity/time assignment are the following:

1. Vary activities, generally allowing for at least two different categories of responses from the students (reading, talking, writing, and so on).

2. Have a standard procedure, like a basic question to be answered, drawn perhaps from the homework or the previous day's lesson, as the initial part of a lesson plan. This can give the students something relevant to do and free the teacher's attention for the procedural chores that invariably cluster at the outset of a class session. Smaller children might go to a "free reading" area or activity center during the initial minutes of a lesson.

3. Don't just list "discussion" on your lesson plan. It might be a better idea to note specifically those questions that should be considered to give sufficient appropriate practice for students. Rarely, if ever, in compliance with the previous suggestions, plan discussions for a whole class period. Students, even at advanced levels, get tired of the same thing, and unless the discussion topic is unusually provocative, an overlong, rambling discussion is likely to occur if stretched over too long a period.

4. Note the names of any particular students you wish to attend to during the lesson, perhaps saving a question for someone you've discovered you have inadvertently been ignoring.

5. A lesson plan can have one or many specific objectives, and a series of lessons can contribute to only one objective. There is no point in being slavish to a "one objective–one lesson plan" correspondence.

6. As in lecturing, it is best to avoid using the lesson plan as a written script. A statement that is read rarely sounds spontaneous. It is best to use some sort of outline in order to note what you wish to say, except in the case of technical statements where precision of language is essential.

Teaching units

A teaching unit is an instructional plan for a period of instruction longer than one class period, usually a week or more. The utility of a teaching unit lies in the framework it provides for long-term planning. Important objectives can be developed systematically over a long time period. Similarly, the teacher can better evaluate his own instruction at the end of this extended period than after a single lesson that may or may not be powerful enough to produce the desired behavior changes in the learners. The development of affective objectives is certainly more suitable in a unit context than in that of a daily lesson plan.

Units of instruction generally are cohesive in terms of topic as well as time. Units may be centered about a particular subtopic in a discipline, "The Short Story" or "The Cell," or they may be organized on a more general thematic basis, "Friends in the Community" or "Leisure-Time Sports." The selection of a topical unit is most common in secondary school classes, where a topic such as the short story would imply a limited set of content, that is, short stories. Another type of unit in an English course might be based on "Prejudice," and content selected could include essay writing, plays, poetry, and the like.

The objectives selected for teaching units should generally be at the higher levels of the cognitive taxonomy and include affective objectives. A unit should also include a chronological plan for implementing the objectives. This plan most economically could consist of a brief description of planned events in the classroom, including notes regarding what both the teachers and students will be doing. These notes should be written in either outline or brief expository form in sufficient detail so that a substitute teacher could understand in general terms what the teacher's instructional plans are.

In planning a unit, it is generally good practice to list all major assignments, homework and in-class. In this way it is possible to verify that all intended practice is provided for the objectives. If the planning of such assignments is deferred until daily lessons are prepared, the incidence of either redundancy or omission is likely to increase.

What basic components should the teacher include in a teaching unit? (1) Provide a brief description of the unit and the type of student population for which it was prepared. (2) Prepare a list of operational objectives that are intended to be attained. If performance standards for the objectives have been established, note them. (3) Describe pre-assessment procedures briefly. (4) Provide a daily account of the major planned classroom events. Describe discussion in terms of major points to be treated. Include classroom assignments. In this chronological portion, the use of learning principles such as appropriate practice, knowledge of results, and so on should be discernible. (5) Describe in detail the manner in which the objectives will be measured. This may be conveniently accomplished by including copies of the tests of the objectives. In lieu of the entire instrument, insert sample items. Also, discuss the method of assessing any attitudinal objectives. (6) Note any unique materials to be used in the unit, such as films, supplementary texts, and exhibits. If the teacher produces a workable unit, the inclusion of all of the above tends to allow his success to be repeated by other teachers who might wish to use his unit.

A unit is more than six weeks' worth of lesson plans. For one thing, it differs from lesson plans by being planned with a higher level of generality. It includes none of the minute-to-minute lesson plan description. The use of a unit should render lesson-plan production simple.

The ultimate utility of a teaching unit is in how it serves a particular teacher. Insistence on detail in unit planning may be excellent for developing the prospective teacher's careful attention to fine points, but it generally results in a teacher's overreacting and abandoning the whole idea of planned instructional events.

Because we strongly recommend that teachers not discard instructional planning because of its time-consuming nature, we have taken a soft-line approach in describing the desirable attributes of any instructional technique such as lecturing or methods of planning lessons. The reason a soft line must be legitimately taken is that there is no real evidence that any given technique is successful with all subject matters, with all teacher personalities, and with all students. There is even little evidence that a particular technique is generalizable to certain teacher types, students, and subject areas.

It is very unlikely that such evidence will be gathered in time to do very much good for this century's teachers. In the absence of conclusive or even partial data on the relationship of presentation techniques to pupil performance, the teacher can do one of two things: (1) use conventional wisdom prescriptively (always have students take notes during lectures); (2) use conventional wisdom descriptively ("Here's a suggested alternative. It may work for you."). If an empirical research approach is used, then at least a given teacher can discover what works in the classroom *for him*.

The Use of Programed Instructional Materials

An alternative that the teacher ought to be able to consider with increasing frequency as the years progress is the use of programed instructional materials. These materials fully exemplify the empirical instructional paradigm advocated in this text. Since they do, programed materials generally will prove to be valuable instructional tools that most teachers can use with profit. A brief examination of programed instructional materials is, therefore, in order.

In the late 1950's programed instruction received its major impetus from the writing of B. F. Skinner, who argued that what had been learned in the animal laboratory had considerable relevance for the classroom and that if we wished to design a systematic scheme for modifying human behavior we had to use reinforcement procedures such as those employed in his laboratory. He urged that the most efficient method for providing subtle reinforcement contingencies was through the use of teaching machines that presented carefully arranged or "programed" instructional materials. Because of Skinner's influence during those early days, the concept of programed instruction came to include three significant characteristics:

1. *Active response* of the student to carefully sequenced instructional materials.
2. The provision of *immediate knowledge of results*, whereby the learner could judge whether his response was correct or incorrect.
3. *Self-pacing*, whereby the student was able to move at his own rate through the instructional program.

Very quickly, programed instructional specialists began to develop materials for simple machines and textbooks that satisfied these three criteria. In the programed textbooks, the student usually wrote down his response in the book and then, by turning a page or moving some kind of simple answer mask, discovered whether his response was correct or incorrect. These features were essentially the same as those provided by the early teaching machines, which were essentially glorified page-turners. They, too, provided an opportunity for the student to make a response, and then by pressing a lever to judge whether his response was correct or incorrect. The real advantage of the machines was that they tended to be somewhat "cheat-proof" because the student was typically unable to modify his answer once it had been made. As the early experimental evidence began to pile up, it became clear that, at least with simple teaching machines, there was no particular advantage of the machine over the textbook, and the programed text became a far more prevalent method of presenting self-instruction materials to the learner.

The early programed texts, subscribing rather thoroughly to a

Skinnerian concept of learning, tended to be based on a *linear* conception of instruction—that is, the student proceeded in a straight line through the small segments or "frames" of the instructional material. The "step size" between frames was extremely small: the student moved from one segment of information to another in exceedingly small steps. In addition, programs tended to be inordinately dull. Many of the early programs, in particular, followed Skinnerian mandates to the point that they included no irrelevant information and almost no attempt to create a positive affect toward the material. Many of the early programers forgot that it was necessary to keep the student "plugged in" to the material in order for him to learn it. As a consequence, a number of educators who came into contact with early programed instructional materials became rather thoroughly disenchanted with the merits of programed instruction.

More recently, a broadened conception of instructional programing has tended to emphasize the *replicability* of the instructional sequence rather than its particular characteristics such as self-pacing, knowledge of results, or active student response. Lumsdaine[1] has offered a generally accepted definition of programed instruction that describes a program as an essentially reproducible set of instructional events that takes responsibility for reliably producing a specified behavior change in the learner. Note that this definition makes no reference to individual characteristics of the material, such as active response, and permits use of a host of presentation procedures. The important thing is that the instructional events be replicable—that is, not dependent on the idiosyncratic and unreproducable behavior of a "live" teacher.

Publishers are now producing programed instructional text materials, often in small-unit or "modular" form, that incorpor-

[1]A. A. Lumsdaine, "Educational Technology, Programed Learning, and Instructional Science," in *Theories of Learning and Instruction*, Sixty-Third Yearbook, National Society for the Study of Education, Part I (Chicago: Distributed by the University of Chicago Press, 1964), p. 385.

ate much of what seemed to be abandoned in the early days of programed instruction—the proper use of color, illustrations, cartoons, and the like, and the many other features that tend to keep students interested in the subject matter. The general tendency originally established in programed instructional materials to produce empirical evidence as to whether the materials accomplished their intended objectives is still being maintained. Thus, the teacher may find that he can select, by consulting an instructor's manual, a set of programed materials that have been demonstrated to accomplish a given kind of behavior change reliably with specified types of learners. If the learners on which the programed materials have been validated tend to correspond to the learners in the teacher's classroom, and the objectives coincide with those he thinks desirable, there is no reason why he should not use the programed instructional materials as a valuable tool in his instructional repertoire.

As more such materials become available, it will be possible to differentiate classroom instruction far more efficiently than the teacher has been able to do in the past; for instead of having to provide some students with "busy work" while he deals with others, the teacher can give the first group programed materials that can be relied upon to teach worthwhile things. The important point is that the teacher keep an open mind regarding the merits of programed instructional material, and, if he happens to view the movement adversely because of an unfortunate encounter with some of the earlier, dull programs, that he continue to examine new programed materials as they appear on the market. A tremendous advantage of current programed materials is that they have been developed on the basis of an empirical instructional model: the programers have commenced with precise objectives and then, through a self-corrective scheme that usually involves many revisions, have developed programs that reliably achieve those objectives. With a collection of tested instructional programs, most teachers will be in a much better position to perform their tasks efficiently.

Indeed, the teacher of the future may be far more of a *selector* of instructional materials than a generator of his own. It may be that the teacher in future decades will have to receive more training in the interpretation of instructor's manuals available with programed materials than in the care and feeding of daily lesson plans. If this latter situation promotes the improved achievement of learners and can relieve the teacher from some of the more time-consuming tasks that programed materials can as readily accomplish, the prospects are really bright for improving the quality of American education.

ADDITIONAL READING

Blount, Nathan S., and Herbert J. Klausmeier, *Teaching in the Secondary School* (New York: Harper & Row, Publishers, 1968).

Cantor, Nathaniel F., *The Dynamics of Learning* (Buffalo: Foster and Stewart, 1946).

De Cecco, John P., *The Psychology of Learning and Instruction: Educational Psychology* (Englewood Cliffs, N.J.: Prentice-Hall, Inc., 1968).

Lumsdaine, A. A., "Educational Technology, Programmed Learning, and Instructional Science," in *Theories of Learning and Instruction*, Sixty-Third Yearbook, National Society for the Study of Education, Part I (Chicago: Distributed by the University of Chicago Press, 1964).

Sanders, Norris M., *Classroom Questions—What Kinds?* (New York: Harper & Row, Publishers, 1966).

8

Classroom
Management

There has been an increasing, and to many, an unsettling influx of industrial language into the educational domain. "Classroom management," if viewed as a euphemism for "disciplinary techniques," could be so assailed. Many teachers are worried about classroom control. In some areas of our country the fear is practical (and physical) as well as theoretical. Teachers do not wish to lose face in the classroom. They must have some attention from their learners if the use of the instructional model herein described is to succeed at all.

"Discipline" as a term is largely punitive. We discipline the rowdies. This discussion is broader than a mere description of punishment for those we've failed. It also considers *prevention* of disorder and therefore is legitimately described as classroom management. How does one avoid classroom difficulties? One doesn't. But one can reduce their incidence and deal with them efficiently when they occur. A traditional homily to offer in these circumstances is the following: "An exciting learning program will preclude discipline problems." This may be so, but since learning programs that excite the interest even of the more unruly students are just those that are least likely to be developed, other classroom-management methods have to be sought. A disclaimer for the rest of this chapter is that most everything that we offer here lacks supporting data. Empirical research pertaining to classroom management is very scarce.

General "Truths"

Some of the most pervasive discipline cases arise when the teacher is unsure of his status in relation to his students. This difficulty might be traced to the teacher's lack of interest in and knowledge of his students. Take a typical middle-class teacher. It has been belabored by many that he is unlikely to be able to identify with the needs of his ghettoed learners. He doesn't understand why they behave as they do, and the students return his ignorance. Why should the students attempt to aid this alien type? Classroom order is *his* problem, not theirs. Confronted with this threatening situation, a new teacher is likely to select either of two inappropriate courses of action. He may become rigid and overstrict with the students, seeing every encounter as a test of his authority (and perhaps of the middle-class values he espouses). By being firm with his students he is preserving the fabric of society. He may also be making life very hard for himself. Another teacher may attempt to become a "true friend" of his students. "Call me Joe, not Mr. Sullivan," he says jovially. He may attempt to use the students' vernacular, which he is likely to do self-consciously. He may be so lenient that he is unable to direct the class's attention when necessary for instructional purposes.

We hope that these horror stories indicate what is felt to be desirable. A teacher must attempt to know his students. If he can attempt to understand some of the problems they are having—those that are typical for their age or frequent in their particular environment—he may be able to anticipate the kinds of difficulty he is likely to encounter and make probable decisions in a rational rather than beleaguered frame of mind. Yet he should, particularly with older students, be reluctant to relinquish completely the responsibility for being the ultimate classroom arbiter.

Much of what goes on in the classroom is a matter of style, this being especially true of the perception the teacher has of "control." To be thoroughly "in control" to some teachers means to dominate all classroom activity. Students are never to interrupt each other, even in discussion, and classroom activity is characterized by a businesslike order. Other teachers feel firmly in control when there is much freedom of movement and talk in the class. An uninitiated observer might think that mayhem rather than learning was the primary outcome of such a class.

Employing a System

Probably the best approach to classroom management involves planned rather than spontaneous decisions made under pressure. If in anger or frustration a teacher sends a student to an administrator for a reprimand, he may feel that the punishment was excessive after he has regained composure. The next time a similar offense occurs, must he give the same treatment to the new culprit? If he does, he is unfair; if he doesn't, he is inconsistent. In many cases, mere anticipation of classroom problems can help him avoid such dilemmas.

If a teacher is going to use a systematic approach to discipline or control problems, how does he decide what to do? Because the area is sparsely researched, a theoretical framework rather than validated specifics is about the best that can be offered. Such a framework is loosely based on B. F. Skinner's reinforcement theory. In nontechnical language, the teacher is the one who controls some reinforcers or rewards for the student. The reinforcers to which the teacher has access are generally weak when compared with familial and peer reinforcers. A child may view the gift of a bicycle from his father, or acceptance into a gang, as more important rewards than a *B* grade from a teacher. However, manipulation of those events that are rewarding to students can still be a great help in preventing or controlling discipline problems. Note that reward, a positive factor, is mentioned and not punishment, a negative stimulus.

The premise of this approach is that appropriate classroom deportment can partially be shaped by the introduction or withholding of rewards. Let's consider an example of how reinforcement practices might depart from more conventional teacher responses to disciplinary problems:

Greg is in your history class and drops his books incessantly. Normally, the teacher might reprimand him and tell him to be more careful. A teacher employing reinforcement principles may choose to ignore Greg and his inveterate clumsiness. Perhaps what Greg wants is attention of any kind, and a reprimand is as good as a comforting word, sometimes better. To decide what to do, a teacher must decide why the pupil is behaving as he is, and then determine whether attention will reinforce the behavior (increase the probability that it will recur). The diagnosis of why the student is behaving in a disorderly fashion may sound clinical, mentalistic, and inconsistent with the "observable" approach taken in this volume. Naturally, most teachers aren't equipped to make valid clinical evaluations of their students; but at least the teacher can attend to the idea that the behavior might possibly be attention-soliciting and thus not react with punishment to every classroom disturbance.

Meaningful rewards

The promise of an *A* or threat or an *F* means little to a student who doesn't think school marks are important. For the same student, however, permission to talk to a friend for five minutes during the class could be very rewarding. Similarly, rather casual commendations to a class such as "You were good students today" may not be so meaningful as a specific remark directed to a particular learner. The way you find out what is really rewarding to students is to find out more about them. It is in the selection of reinforcers that the teacher might unwittingly assume that his own value system is shared by his students.

Explaining the rules

It is best to let students know what is appropriate classroom behavior in your class. If gum chewing is not permitted, let the students know rather than wait for an unsuspecting gum chewer to be snared by your hidden rules. Tell the class the limits you have set. Students will sometimes be surprisingly willing to comply.

Avoiding character judgments

Another general rule in classroom management and relations with students is to refrain from making negative judgments about a student's character. An incident of misbehavior, or even a series of them, is just that—an event. A teacher might say, "John, you broke a rule" or "Your talking is annoying me and the class," but he should not say, "You are a bad boy" or "Why do you always cause trouble?" It takes a little practice to excise the name-calling tendencies that inhabit many of us, but such tendencies should be eliminated. The teacher should not impugn the worth of a single student. We cannot cite strong empirical evidence to support this suggestion, but the parable of Mary Magdalene might be cogent for some.

The following pages provide a collection of actions you could

take on those infrequent occasions when your skillful manipulation of reinforcers has been inadequate and your students
are behaving inappropriately. Perhaps most of these suggestions are not consonant with your personality style, but one or
two may prove useful to you. You might wish to try some of
these out to see how they work for you.

Incident-Related Problems

Sometimes problems will occur that are related to an action
by a particular student or groups of students. Such problems
can be classed as incident-related since they may be relatively
isolated.

Closing in

If a student begins to act up, one generally useful technique
is to move closer to him. The teacher's presence can be intimidating and allow the student to desist from his disruptive
behavior without direct comment by the teacher. Should the
student develop a pronounced tendency toward misbehavior,
moving the student's place close to the teacher's desk could
have the desired inhibiting effect. (If the student has a "crush"
on the teacher, however, this would be an unfortunate use of
reinforcement techniques.)

Signals

When a student is mildly misbehaving, the teacher can signal
him that he is under surveillance. Such signals might be a
finger-snap, a knowing glance, or a wave of the hand. These
signals should help the miscreant to control himself, but should
be used in a way that does not interrupt the activities of the
class. This means that the sign given is a *little* one, and not
disruptive in itself, such as book slamming or handclapping
may be. When a teacher makes a tympanic scene over a dis-

cipline incident, he removes the possibility of the learner's controlling his own behavior. Furthermore, if the teacher is very dramatic, his actions in themselves can be reinforcing to the learners, and they may misbehave just to get the teacher to put on a show.

Humor

Sometimes, when the incident is small, the teacher might well choose to make light of a student's misbehavior in a non-sarcastic way. By calling attention to the problem in a humorous manner, the teacher maintains good will and gives warning to the offender that he knows what is afoot. The humor used, however, ought not be too polished because the class's response to such a scintillating routine might be more disruptive than the actions of the misbehaving student.

Ignoring

Ignoring, not to be confused with ignorance, can often be purposefully used in mild disciplinary situations. To practice this method, the teacher must have the flexibility not to make every infraction punishable by his acknowledgment. In certain cases, ignoring misbehavior can work out well; for instance, when the teacher suspects the student is desirous of attention and is acting up so the teacher will deal with him. If the teacher feels that the problem will remain isolated to the single student, misbehavior can be ignored. But if the probability is that other students will be either disturbed or enticed by the situation, the teacher had better take some action.

The out-of-sight technique

The teacher can use the out-of-sight technique when he is confronted by disruptive behavior that is clearly out of the students' control. The most prominent example of this sort of behavior is the situation when adolescents, usually girls, get the giggles. Such attacks are infectious and often persist even when the offender herself wishes they would stop. To become punitive in such a situation is pointless, since the student is generally as anxious to stop as the teacher is to have her do so. An effective remedy might be to allow a student in such a predicament to leave the room. Such action should be taken permissively rather than punishingly. There should be no hint of permanent exile. Simply, the student is being allowed to remove himself to an environment where he can regain his self-control and then return to class.

General Class Disturbance

Another set of discipline problems and their associated remedies can be grouped together because they all tend to involve a larger proportion of the class than incident-related problems. These general class disturbances will usually be more symptomatic of pervasive problems than those in the first category.

Open discussion

When the overall level of misbehavior increases in a classroom, teachers are often dumbfounded. They may reevaluate their actions and instruction and be unable to suggest any hypotheses to explain the students' actions. The use of a free, open discussion with the students can be very helpful. If the teacher can set one up, such a discussion can provide a welcome opportunity for students to air their grievances. They may indicate a general lack of perceived purpose for the ensuing instruction. They may object to procedures that the teacher feels to be desirable or at least innocuous. A teacher could start such a discussion by clearly saying that he has noticed difficulties occurring in the class and hopes the students will aid him in his search to end the problem. An important rule is that the teacher must *not* be defensive as the students begin to discuss things they would like to see changed. If the teacher even attempts to explain why he used certain approaches, the students may feel that their opinions are valueless. The teacher's role is to listen, acceptingly, to what the students have to say. One constraint here is that he should generally not allow the students to indulge in discussions of shortcomings of other teachers. After the session is over and all gripes duly noted, the teacher does not have to incorporate all student suggestions into his subsequent lesson plans; but he may be able to make a number of concessions that will make the classroom atmosphere somewhat more amenable to learning than before.

Explaining the procedure

Sometimes disciplinary problems are directly related to the students' inability to perform the task assigned to them. Such difficulty typically arises when the teacher assumes the students to possess a skill they do not have. Typical of such situations are the problems that often surround discussion or committee assignments. The students will become disruptive primarily because they don't know how to organize a committee for productive work or to participate meaningfully in a discussion. Many times all the teacher has to do is provide some guidelines for what is expected of the students. In a slightly different way, behavior problems that seem to be invariably attached to unusual classroom events, such as movies, library excursions, fire drills, and field trips, may be attributable to the students' need for reminders regarding what procedures will be used and what standards are expected. Such a review preceding a trip or drill can prevent a good many harrowing experiences for the teacher.

Teacher analysis

Sometimes a class will misbehave rather continuously and the teacher has a good idea what is causing the disturbance.

Perhaps the students are keyed up for a school event. Perhaps a community incident or current controversy is influencing their behavior. Sometimes, by simply saying, "I know X is bothering you, but let's try to concentrate," the teacher can alleviate the problem, since perhaps the students themselves hadn't pinpointed the stimulus for their restive actions.

Restructuring

When classroom disturbances increase in frequency, one immediate course of action, short of an open-discussion session, is to *change* what you are doing immediately. If a discussion is getting out of hand, switch and perhaps give individuals summaries to read in textbooks, or have students read in books of their choice, or play a game, or take five minutes off. The teacher should be responsive to obvious inadequacies in his instructional plans and, instead of persevering through a rather dull lesson, revise on the spot. The justification for doing so is clear if one attends at all to affective as well as cognitive outcomes. Forcing students to do work that obviously bores them will not likely result in positive consequences.

In restructuring, be careful to avoid always providing an amusing alternative, for students could catch on and systematically misbehave so they can have "fun and games."

Last Recourse Techniques

There are instances when, because all else has failed, the teacher may have to try certain last recourse procedures. As we indicate below, these techniques should be used sparingly to be at all effective.

Appeal

Sometimes a teacher will say, "Please be quiet." This utterance will occasionally do the trick, and the students will become well-mannered, attentive people. However, when appeal is used frequently, it casts the teacher into the role of supplicant at the students' mercy. When this technique is used over and over, the students will tend not to be merciful.

Restraint

When a student is disruptive in a physical way or is threatening the safety of other members of the group, he must be physically restrained. Such action is preventive and protective and should be clearly differentiated from use of physical punishment.

Punishment

There is very little evidence that punishment works well with people, whether it be punishing by removing privileges or punishing by adding negative consequences. Of corporal punishment, there is nothing good to say. It is a brutish indictment of the failure of the teacher. Protestations that this type of punishment is "good for kids" is not accepted by any respectable clinician. Corporal punishment may provide a release for the teacher's pent-up frustrations; a workout in the school gym is a preferable alternative.

Teachers who feel drawn to the use of physical punishment might well introspect on the reason they like it so much. Dependency on such techniques may stem, aside from a serious aberration, from the same instructional laziness that blames only students for poor test performance.

Another type of punishment that does not seem particularly defensible is the association of more school work with poor deportment. The assignment of fifty or one thousand "I will always . . ." written drills are pointless enough; but there is real danger in consistent association of more homework or longer essays with misbehaving. School work should be invested with positive or, at worst, neutral tones and *never* equated with punishment. Quick recall of the affective taxonomy might help convince you.

Summary

The discussion in this chapter is admittedly not based on evidence-supported verities. The area of classroom management is one of the least carefully studied areas of education. In spite of this, the teacher can still adopt an empirical posture in dealing with pupil misbehavior, either present or potential. He can try out some of the experience-based techniques described here—try them out to see if they work for him in his situation. If they do, fine. If they don't, he should try something else. He should keep searching for a personal collection of management procedures that yield the kind of classroom order he wishes.

ADDITIONAL READING

Sheviakov, George, and Fritz Redl, *Discipline for Today's Children & Youth* (Washington, D.C.: ASCD National Education Assoc., 1956).

Webster, Staten W., *Discipline in the Classroom* (San Francisco, Calif.: Chandler Publishing Company, 1968).

9

The Evaluation
of Instruction

If a teacher is committed to improvement of his instruction, he must make some evaluation of the success of his teaching in order to know where modifications should be made. Students must also be evaluated. A strange quirk of instructional methodology is that these two critical processes are generally considered separately. Our position is that evaluation of teachers should not disassociate these two tasks but rather should depend *primarily* on the record of achievements that teachers produce in their learners. A problem, then, is for a teacher to be able to design measurement instruments that properly reflect the objectives he is trying to achieve.

Tests can be put to many purposes. Standardized tests are frequently used for "selection," for example, to determine where a child "fits" in reading or arithmetic when he is compared with other children of his age or grade. Such tests are not appropriate bases for teacher evaluation, since the tests probably do not measure the particular objectives that a given teacher has. It simply isn't fair to use nationally normed, comprehensive tests for the specific purpose of evaluating teachers.

These tests are called *norm-referenced* or *standardized* tests because the values they ascribe to different performances are interpreted in terms of some normative population of students. Scores are often reported in percentiles, stanines, or standard scores, all of which use the group average as a point of reference. Most commercially available tests are of this type.

Certainly there is nothing wrong in general with using an average as a test referent, but standardized tests typically do a disservice to the accurate evaluation of instruction. In the design of the test items used in such tests the item writer is extremely anxious to produce heterogeneous scores so that the test can discriminate among those who complete it, otherwise the test would be of little use for selection purposes. Items for such tests should enable an extremely bright student to get one score and a bright student to get a slightly lower score. In order to reflect such minor differences in performance, these tests may use items that are not always very representative of the skill being tested. Many items must be particularly difficult in order to produce a high enough "test ceiling" so that there would be a good spread in student performance. Thus even when a teacher may have done a thoroughly commendable job of teaching a given concept, this effort might not be reflected in the absolute value of the students' scores on norm-referenced tests.

If a teacher wishes to have an adequate basis for judging the quality of his instruction, he should use tests that accurately and representatively reflect his objectives. How can he assure this accuracy? Unless he has access to prepared items, he must get into the business of writing tests himself. Tests that the teacher produces have the advantage of being right on the instructional target—that is, essentially equivalent to that teacher's instructional goals. The performance of students, therefore, can be used to make valid judgments regarding the performance of the teacher, generally in terms of the previously established class minimal level of student performance. Tests designed exclusively to measure the objectives taught are called *criterion-referenced* tests. Their purpose, unlike that of norm-referenced tests, is not to make differentiations among achievement levels of various students, but to measure accurately how well each student has attained stated objectives. In a sense, then, norm-referenced tests are *relative* measures because an individual's score is interpreted in relationship to the scores of others. Criterion-referenced tests are *absolute* measures because an individual's score is interpreted in relationship to a fixed criterion, not the scores of other individuals.

Criterion-referenced tests are usually employed at the conclusion of an instructional sequence. However, the same principles that go into their construction are used in tests given for pretesting criterion behaviors or for measuring en route behaviors.

Planning a Test

Tests should enable a teacher to gather observations about the students' ability with respect to the instructional objective. As we indicated earlier, a test may consist of either a *student product*, such as a term paper, a spelling test, or an art project, or a record of *student behavior*, such as a student's observed ability to sing a scale, make a speech, or throw a ball. The form the test takes—whether it calls for product or behavior—depends on the objective that the teacher has originally stated.

Most tests involve pupil products. Behavior tests are valuable, however, and should often be used when the *method* of making the product as well as the product itself is of interest. Behavior records are usually the best way to measure affective objectives—for example, to see if students have learned to cooperate on group projects.

Tests can be given under clearly manipulated or under natural conditions.

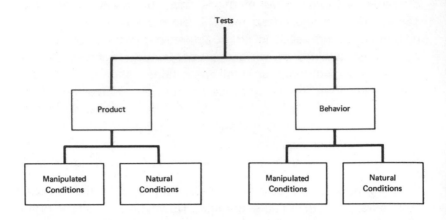

Most tests are administered under manipulated conditions—
that is, the teacher deliberately sets up the stimulus condition.
"Solve any two of three problems," "Spell zebra," or "Swim 50
yards," are directions given by the teacher to indicate that a
particular kind of response is desired. Tests under natural conditions consist largely of data gathering while the learner has
no idea that he is being tested. Observations of students working with peers, inspection of grammar used in the personal
letters students write to friends, determination of the number
of students electing to enroll on related topics—all are examples of using natural test situations. Natural conditions should
be used when the teacher wishes to determine the way a student really feels about something—that is, his tendency to behave in a particular way when he has not been cued by the
teacher's directions or presence. To find out if students were
stimulated by a particular topic the teacher could, for example,
(1) ask the students directly, (2) see how many library books
they chose on the topic during free reading time. The second
measure shows more clearly the unbiased choices that the students make. Learner responses in natural conditions most accurately reflect affective objectives. The majority of tests,

however, are more direct in their intent and effect on the students. Learner responses in manipulated situations measure cognitive objectives, and since these form the basis of most school instruction, some discussion regarding the desirable attributes of these tests can be profitable.

A test under manipulated conditions should provide a *representative* sample of a student's behavior with respect to a particular skill or ability. Test items, generally, do not *exhaustively* measure the student's achievement. If a pupil at the conclusion of first grade is supposed to be able to read 350 words, the teacher usually does not test the child on all of these words at the end of the year. Usually the time, patience, or attention span isn't sufficient to do so. Instead he uses a test that *samples* the entire set of words. If this portion, or sample, is to be representative, it should have certain qualities. First, it should contain enough words so that a good idea of the child's reading ability is obtained. If the test consisted of only two words, a child might do poorly just because the items selected were not representative, but perhaps were particularly difficult for him. The test will be *more* representative as the number of items included approaches the total number of items possible. In the word-recognition example, a test of twenty words is a better estimate of the child's ability than a test of two words. In general, the longer the test the better representation it gives of the total content to which the objective applies. (A test that is extraordinarily long may not, because of pupil fatigue factors, be a very good measure of anything.) Taking into account what you know about the attention span of your learners, fashion a test that has a sufficient number of items to give a representative measure of the instructional objectives.

How does one select the representative items? One could, if he had to, specify all content to which his objective applies. A teacher can often do this when he is teaching a specified list of words, terms, concepts, or problems. He could generate all two-digit addition combinations and define *all*, or the *uni-*

verse, of the content to which his objective is directed. However, if one were teaching a student to determine the theme of an English lyric, it would be an arduous and largely impossible task to specify all the different lyric poems one could use to test the objective.

In the case where one can specify all the content implied in the objective, the best way of choosing specific items for inclusion on a test is to use *random* procedures. By flipping a coin, placing items into a hat and selecting, or using a table of random numbers and choosing items whose numbers occur first, one can constitute a representative test. Such a test is eminently fair, since every item has the same chance to be used on the test. It is unlikely that the test is systematically biased towards being too hard or too easy. Performance on it would indicate fairly the success the teacher has had with the objective.

Tests for which all items cannot be conveniently identified and randomly sampled as above should still be representative. If a twelfth-grade English teacher wishes students to write a book report, he should select books that are not peculiar or strange and thus bias the results he gets. Similarly, he should probably not select *Unca Donald's Mystery* because it would probably be too easy for his students. When making such a choice, the teacher simply has to use his own good sense.

Item Sampling

While it is true that the teacher must give all students a test comprised of the same items if he wishes to use the test for judging his own instruction *and* grading the students, he need not do so if he is only assessing the quality of his instruction. An approach to testing in which different students receive different items permits the teacher to test a far greater range of objectives, with more items, and in less time. Suppose, for example, that you had six basic objectives for a ten-week unit and seven secondary objectives. Each of the objectives is measured by ten multiple-choice items. Now if you give a sixty-item test to all youngsters covering the basic objectives, you may have only ten minutes left in the examination period, certainly not enough time for another seventy items. You can, however, add seven items to each student's test, but they can be *different* from student to student. Depending on your class size, this means that you might have only three or four pupils responding to a given item. However, you can get a total class-performance estimate based on the percentage of items answered correctly per objective. You would grade your students, of course, only on their responses to the sixty common items. For the remaining items, you grade only yourself.

Types of Test Items

Test items fall into two major classifications. Either they call for the student to select his answers from alternatives, or they call for him to construct his answers himself. A multiple-choice test requires a selected response. Essay writing is a constructed response.

Selected-Response Items

Selected-response tests come in many different varieties, such as true-false, five-alternative multiple choice, and matching items. They are advantageous because they are easy to score and save much time. Further, they have great interscorer reliability since judges marking or grading selected-response tests will customarily give the same score to the same paper. Selected-response tests can be used to measure behavior at any level of the cognitive taxonomy except, perhaps, synthesis. Furthermore, since the time devoted to any one item is relatively brief, a large number of items can be included in a given test, thereby promoting a generally representative test. Disadvantages of selected-response tests are the excessive time they take to prepare and also the guessing factor in answering, which is impossible to ignore.

TRUE-FALSE, OR BINARY CHOICE, ITEMS.   An item that asks the student to agree or disagree with a statement—that is, to label it as true or false—is one of the poorer forms of selected-response test items. It is difficult to build in relative degrees of truth or falsity in such items. Further, they tend to encourage the teacher to lift statements from the text or from lecture notes, thereby promoting memorization activity on the part of the student.

The trouble with such an item form is the difficulty of selecting meaningful items that aren't excessively obvious. Because most things in life are not absolute, a test-wise student will mark "False" whenever he sees "always," "never," or "only" as modifiers in a statement. Similarly, when a statement uses less extreme modifiers, and notes possible exceptions, students tend to mark it as "True." Such tests generally measure only the lower regions of cognitive behavior.

Items in this same class, other than True-False, might be any binary categorization task, such as deciding if a given chemical combination is a mixture or a compound. An obvious problem in any type of binary choice item is the high proportion of correct answers attributable to guessing.

MULTIPLE-CHOICE ITEMS.   Another popular item form is the multiple-choice response, where the stem presents an incomplete sentence or question and alternative completing phrases or answers are provided from which the student makes a choice. Such items can test the student's understanding of a concept by asking him to select the answer that exhibits all of a certain number of attributes.

Writing multiple-choice questions is not easy. One should, for instance, present alternatives that are in the same class of responses. Examine the following item:

La mesa is a:
  a. chair
  b. table
  c. desk
  d. "I pledge allegiance to the flag."

One suspects that "d" is misplaced. Similarly, one must take care that the alternatives are not so doltish as to give an inordinately clear cue for the right answer. For example:

Columbus discovered America in:
  a. 1964
  b. 1947
  c. 1492
  d. 3

Most of the wrong answers are here easily identifiable.

The teacher should be careful that the stem part of the item is rather long in relation to the alternatives. Note the problem with this item:

In the assigned novel, the hero's favorite poem is:
  a. Tyger! Tyger! burning bright
      In the forests of the night,
      What immortal hand or eye
      Could frame thy fearful symmetry? . . .
  b. Had we but world enough, and time,
      This coyness, Lady, were no crime.
      We would sit down and think which way
      To walk and pass our long love's day. . . .
  c. The sea is calm tonight,
      The tide is full, the moon lies fair

Upon the straits;—on the French coast the light
Gleams and is gone; the cliffs of England stand,
Glimmering and vast, out in the tranquil bay. . . .

d. The curfew tolls the knell of parting day,
    The lowing herd winds slowly o'er the lea,
The plowman homeward plods his weary way,
    And leaves the world to darkness and to me. . . .

When the student has to read extended alternatives such as these, his progress through the test is slowed.

The construction of multiple-choice items is almost a technology unto itself. Consult the references given at the close of the chapter for more detailed treatments of this important topic.

Constructed-Response Items

Constructed-response items measure another major class of learner behavior. These items or situations include all instances when the student actually does something or prepares something, for example, performs a dance, completes an art project, or compiles a term paper. Constructed responses can demonstrate achievement of objectives at all levels of the cognitive taxonomy and of most objectives in the psychomotor and affective domains. Constructed responses allow students to display creative or novel solutions to problems. They permit students to demonstrate their ability to organize their work, as in essays or term papers, and to indicate a level of understanding of different topics. Constructed-response items or test situations are generated in much less time than selected-response items. However, they do have certain salient flaws. In most cases, the time it takes to score each answer is extended. When a teacher designs a test that calls for a high proportion of written, constructed responses, he had better set aside a considerable amount of time for correcting papers.

Also, the reliability of scoring a constructed-response item will invariably be lower than for selected-response items. Two different people might view a particular solution to an equation in two vastly different ways. One person might focus only on the correctness of the answer, while another might take into account the procedure the student used. *Even a single teacher might change his standards of grading from one student's paper to another as the time spent on grading expands.* This problem can be somewhat mitigated by establishing precise criteria to help the teacher make decisions more objectively about students answers, but it cannot be totally surmounted.

An additional shortcoming of items or situations calling for constructed responses is the testing time these items generally require of the learner. When a written response is solicited instead of a simple selection indicated by a mark on an answer sheet, more time per question is required of the learner. This time increase, in turn, must reduce the total number of items that can be measured, and the fewer the items observed, the less representative the test is. A number of different constructed-item formats can be used in tests. Each has its own delights and pitfalls.

FILL-IN ITEMS. Fill-in items generally are scored quickly and marked reliably, for example, "Florida is a (an) _____." Usually there is a limited number of acceptable responses to a fill-in question. It is most often used to measure the lower levels of cognitive behavior, such as recall, where a response of just one or two terms would be correct. When preparing fill-in items, be careful not to give cues for the right answer by the context of the stem portion of the question. Also avoid giving more formal cues such as grammatical prompts, length of line provided, or matching number of line segments to number of letters in the called-for word, for example, "President _ _ _ _ was the second president of the United States."

SHORT-ANSWER ITEMS. Short-answer items pose questions

that in many ways function similarly to fill-in items. Again the responses called for are often rather limited, but higher level objectives can be tested by this approach. The shorter the answer required, however, the more reliably the answer can be scored. In scoring both fill-in and short-answer tests, a tentative scoring guide should be prepared in advance with all allowable responses stipulated.

ESSAY EXAMINATIONS.   Essay questions, because of the time they take to answer, should call for higher level cognitive behavior. However, consistent with representative measurement, it is usually wiser to include a few shorter essay items than one very long essay question. The nature of the question should be carefully considered. One of the prevalent problems with essay questions is the lack of specificity with which these questions are phrased. If the teacher has specific objectives, it is reasonable that the questions he asks of students must be precise and that a relatively specific question is necessary to elicit the class of answers sought.

In reading and scoring essay questions, a certain number of rules should be followed. The most important rule is to establish criteria by which the essay or other product is to be judged. The statement of clear objectives radically improves the position of the teacher who uses essay questions, but explicated limits describing what student responses must have in them are essential. Even in subject-matter fields where such descriptions of criterion performance are possible, teachers rarely employ them. If a teacher has an objective that the students be able to prepare a term paper in a history class, the teacher should be able to state what basic characteristics the paper should include. If a teacher cannot describe any attributes that a student's paper should exhibit, the teacher is in an extra-ordinarily untenable position. How can the teacher purport that his instructional efforts have been effective if he cannot describe at least some of the ways in which the results of his instruction can be observed?

With objectives in which the outcome is artistic or expressive rather than cognitive, the teacher's problem is further complicated. Since the outcomes seem largely a reflection of the student's talents rather than of the teacher's ability, the teacher may elect to view his activity as "noninstructional" and not attempt to apply judgments. If, however, the teacher feels that the papers or objects produced by students who *have* been taught should be different from those of a similar group of students who *have not* been exposed to this instruction, then the teacher should attempt to evaluate the effects of his teaching. He should ask himself, "How would I expect the student's work to differ if I had not 'taught' him?" The answer to this question could provide the framework for the establishment of basic criteria for evaluating student responses.

The entire area of artistic expression is controversial. There are those who argue that the art product cannot be evaluated at all. Some might say that the *execution* of the object (Does the collage adhere, or the pottery crack?) can be evaluated, others that satisfaction with artistic expression is only possible for the artist himself. The "doing" of the act is all that counts. This position is, of course, antithetical to the systematic approach proposed in this book; yet such a view can be reconciled with our type of model. All the teacher has to do is to distinguish between classroom events that are the consequence of his instruction and those that transcend his area of measurable influence. In most classes and for most objectives, some expectations of the attributes of student responses should be described. But for those objectives not so describable, the teacher should recognize that he is *not teaching*, that the sequence is not *instructional*, and that his role has radically switched from instructor of a class of responses to custodian of a wide range of unpredictable outcomes. In the latter role, it is difficult for the teacher to *improve* the technique he uses in the classroom. And if most of what the teacher does is not instructional, and therefore not within his realm of *responsibility*, he ought to feel more than casually queasy about the utility of the time he spends in the classroom.

What are some of the specifics to keep in mind when marking or evaluating a student's constructed answer or project? First, it is often suggested that when there are many essay questions answered by each student, the teacher should read all the responses to the first question first, then go on to the second question and read all student answers to it, and so on. The reasons for this procedure are sound, even though the paper shuffling is considerable. By reading all of the answers to one question together, the teacher reduces the chance that a student who writes a good answer to question number one will receive an inflatedly good mark on the second question regardless of his response.

Second, using the basic criteria established, the teacher should attempt to rate the papers in terms of *how well* they approximate the stated criteria. This process is substantially different from the usual essay-grading practice where papers are compared *to each other* and not judged with respect to a particular objective and criterion. Use of criterion-referenced evaluation sometimes disturbs teachers who are interested in fostering divergent responses. But the distress can be readily dispelled by encouraging the preparation of objectives and items that allow a considerable range of responses.

A good teacher, then, would not set up an essay item such as "What is the significance of *Moby Dick*?" and accept only an answer that included the statement that Moby Dick represented "nature," or "evil," or "power." A more acceptable essay item might be: "Write an essay describing three possible interpretations of *Moby Dick* (or any novel) and defend the interpretation that seems most reasonable to you."

Criteria: 1. Each interpretation must discuss the protagonist's role in the major conflict of the novel.

2. Justifications of selected interpretation must cite evidence in the text.

So it is possible to apply criteria to the judgment of essay responses without the implicit insistence on answers that coincide with the teacher's own ideas.

Interpreting Test Results

What happens after tests are scored? Presumably, the teacher is in a position to evaluate the utility of the instructional sequence. When students do well, he will generally be satisfied. (His contentment is justified if he pretested students at the outset and found them without the competencies measured.) If he has produced the intended change in the learner, at a level approaching what he had previously determined as a performance standard, he should seek ways to make himself even more efficient. He might raise the criterion levels that he originally set, either by requiring more of individual students, or by expecting more students in the class to meet the minimal level, or by doing both. He may wish to add more objectives to his course or to substitute more complex objectives for simple ones. At any rate, his task is pleasant and he can be somewhat at peace. The teacher who has poor results on tests has bigger problems. First, he must resist the desire to place the bulk of responsibility for the unhappy outcome on the students. The fact that unsatisfactory performance occurs is more often an indictment of the teacher's poor planning or implementation of instruction (or both) than it is the students' fault. Once a teacher accepts responsibility for his students' performance, he can begin to find ways to improve. Among the problems that might have adversely affected pupil learning are the following; hypothetical actions that may help alleviate these problems are given for each:

Problem 1:   Prerequisite behaviors not measured.
Action: Modify pretest to include prerequisite behaviors; give remedial instruction where necessary.

Problem 2: En route behaviors not achieved.

Action: Have more frequent learner-performance assessments and reteaching cycles.

Problem 3: Sequence incorrectly analyzed. Relevant prerequisites and en route behaviors omitted. Order of instruction inappropriate.

Action: Reanalyze objectives. Vary the component behaviors practiced or the order in which instruction occurs, or both. Use pupil data, post-tests, and quizzes on en route behaviors for clues.

Problem 4: Insufficient appropriate practice.

Action: Plan for more appropriate practice in general or allow greater proportion of time for equivalent practice.

Problem 5: Student attention to task poor.

Action: Include more activities designed to reinforce attending behaviors.

Problem 6: Test items not representative.

Action: Obtain colleagues' opinions of test items; revise the test. Inspect pattern of student responses to determine if certain incorrect responses recur. Check instruction on this point as well.

Certainly these hypotheses for action are not exhaustive, but they do provide a basic framework for the revision process. If hypotheses such as these can be explored and rejected, the possibility exists that you might have had a class with pervasive learning disorders, but it is not likely. After your attempt to implement any of the actions suggested by the hypotheses, your next instructional foray ought to be more successful.

Grading

What does a teacher do when it is time to affix grades on report cards? If he is a successful teacher, he must give many good grades. The myth of the normal distributions, with grades distributed roughly as they appear in the first diagram below, must be discarded.

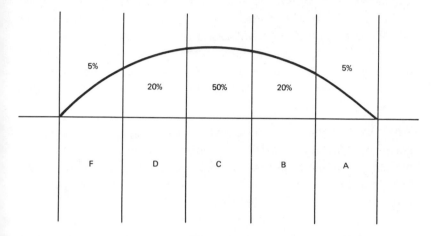

Distributions for criterion-referenced tests preceded by relatively effective instruction should look more like this:

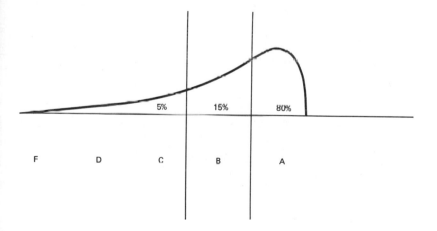

Such distributions do not coincide with administrative expectations, but if instruction is successful we must expect to reward learners for doing well. One possible solution is a pass-fail basis for grading. Students who succeed at a stated level of achievement could simply be "passed" and the A to F assignments avoided. However, if such a scheme is not acceptable to the school in which you teach, you could conceivably use the achievement of different types of objectives as a basis for grading. Students who achieved the most difficult objectives would receive the best grades. With individualized plans for instruction becoming a reality, such a grading format might be possible.

When the teacher is unsuccessful, when most students fail to achieve well on the post-test, grading problems are even more pressing. For example, is it fair to penalize students who perform poorly for what may be a deficiency in your pedagogy? If no student meets your criterion limits, do you fail everyone? We suggest that the answers to both questions are *no*, but there is little else to offer. Grading is very subjective. Teachers are forced to make judgments by comparing students to one another, and any such decision is bound to be shaky. How can a teacher say that Sally is a *B*+ while Mitchell is an *A*−? Is there so much difference between them? The problem is compounded by the realization that the grades that are recorded can radically affect someone's life. A *C* instead of a *B* could keep someone out of the college he has planned on. A *D* might help place a child in a "slow" classroom.

All that a teacher can sensibly do is recognize that grades are very arbitrary, for in many cases the tests and the objectives they reflect are not immutable. He must establish beforehand as many explicit criteria for grading as possible. And he must try to use them. But be gentle.

ADDITIONAL READING

Ebel, Robert L., *Measuring Educational Achievement* (Englewood Cliffs, N.J.: Prentice-Hall, 1965).

The Evaluation of Teaching, A Report of the Second Pi Lambda
Theta Catena (Washington, D.C.: Pi Lambda Theta, 1967).

Popham, W. James, "The Performance Test: A New Approach to
the Assessment of Teaching Proficiency," *The Journal of
Teacher Education*, XIX, No. 2 (Summer 1968).

Scriven, Michael, "The Methodology of Evaluation," *AERA Monograph Series on Curriculum Evaluation* (Chicago: Rand McNally
& Company, 1967).

Wood, Dorothy Adkins, *Test Construction: Development and Interpretation of Achievement Tests* (Columbus, Ohio: Charles E. Merrill
Books, Inc., 1960).

10

The Teacher as an Experimenter

Throughout this book we have been advocating that the teacher constantly test the effect of his instructional decisions according to the way learners behave at the close of an instructional sequence. Through this emphasis upon empirical evidence, an instructor becomes a *teacher-empiricist* who is capable of systematic improvement. But some teachers may wish to move even beyond this altogether commendable stance—move beyond it in order to become a *teacher-experimenter*. What is the essential difference between the teacher-empiricist and the teacher-experimenter? As we indicated, the teacher-empiricist is constantly looking to empirical results—that is, data based on pupil behavior—in order to judge the effectiveness of his instructional decisions. The teacher-experimenter, in addition to this activity, actually designs small-scale classroom experiments in which he tests hypotheses in a relatively controlled environment. Whereas the teacher-empiricist judges the adequacy of *one* particular instructional treatment he has designed, the teacher-experimenter may wish to contrast respective merits of *two or more* alternative treatments in order to determine the one that works best for him.

149

We have argued throughout this text that to be a thoroughly professional practitioner a teacher must employ a systematic approach to instruction such as the four-component model we advocate. If the professional teacher wishes to become even more skilled, he must have ways of increasing his insight regarding instructional matters. There are two fairly obvious courses of action that the teacher can pursue in order to improve his conversance with potentially helpful instructional variables. The first of these involves his consumption of the research results produced by others, the second involves his actual conduct of small-scale experimental studies in his own classroom.

The Research Consumer

Any skilled practitioner in a respectable field of specialization is conversant with the theoretical and research literature of his field. He can consult specialized journals in order to become aware of "cutting edge" thoughts and newly discovered, evidence-supported principles. It is unfortunate that so many teachers are unable, largely because they cannot comprehend the basic language of the educational researcher, to read the research literature of their field with even rudimentary understanding.

In the course of their inservice education, it is highly desirable that teachers complete college courses dealing with research procedures and with statistical methodology. They can then be enlightened consumers of the educational researchers' efforts. A teacher should subscribe to such publications as the *American Journal of Educational Research, The Journal of Educational Research*, and *The Journal of Experimental Education* and should be able to read them with comprehension. Frequently, the investigations reported in these journals can suggest a variety of improved instructional practices. Then too, reviews of educational research such as in *The Handbook of*

Research on Teaching and *The Encyclopedia of Educational Research*, published under the auspices of the American Educational Research Association, have a wealth of potentially useful suggestions for teachers. The teacher who is interested in learning more about research and statistics can gain the knowledge by attending either regular degree courses or extension courses; or, if that's impossible, he can consult the ever increasing collection of readable texts on the subject.[1]

The Hypothesis Tester

A second method by which the teacher can continually feed new ideas into his instructional repertoire is by conducting small-scale classroom experiments. These experiments will typically be designed to discover the relationship between some kind of instructional treatment (the independent variable) and learner attainment of instructional objectives (the dependent variable). For instance, the teacher might wish to investigate the effects of two methods of providing in class knowledge of results (immediate versus delayed) on student performance in a mathematics examination. In this instance the treatment variable would be immediate versus delayed knowledge of results. It is called a variable because there are two identifiably different categories of the characteristic. The dependent variable would be student performance on the examination. It is called a variable because students will obtain different scores on the measure. The teacher may wish to test a specific hypothesis such as the following: *With immediate knowledge of results, learner performance will be significantly superior than with delayed knowledge of results.* If the teacher can conduct a small-scale experiment that can test this hypothesis, it is obvious that in future instructional situations the results of the

[1]An example, offered with thorough bias by the elder author, is W. James Popham, *Educational Statistics: Use and Interpretation* (Harper & Row Publishers, New York, 1967). The younger author prefers William L. Hays, *Statistics for Psychologists* (Holt, Rinehart & Winston, Inc., 1963).

experiment, depending upon whether the hypothesis was confirmed, would lead to more frequent use of immediate (or delayed) knowledge of results. There are all sorts of other independent variables that the teacher might wish to study. Characteristically, these will be in the form of treatment variables —that is, instructional procedures—since treatment variables can be readily manipulated by an instructor. By working with manipulable variables such as different varieties of an instructional treatment, the teacher can identify those particular procedures that result in improved student achievement in his class.

Many teachers who set out to engage in classroom experimentation (sometimes loosely referred to as "action research") will use research designs that are not adequate for evaluating the impact of an independent variable upon a dependent variable. The teacher may have a nodding acquaintance with research procedures and, unfortunately, may nod when he should have been shaking his head. For instance, some teachers introduce a treatment such as a particular variety of homework exercises, then, after this treatment, measure the performance of the class. This is referred to by researchers as a *One-Shot Case Study*.[2]

TREATMENT ▶ MEASUREMENT

Figure 1. *One-Shot Case Study*

The One-Shot Case Study has obvious disadvantages, and the teacher should feel very uncomfortable about any inferences

[2]The designs treated in this chapter have been well explicated at a more advanced level in Donald T. Campbell and Julian C. Stanley, *Experimental and Quasi-Experimental Designs for Research* (Chicago: Rand McNally & Company, 1967). Because of the widespread use of the Campbell and Stanley treatise, the designs treated here will be the same as the ones given by those authors.

made regarding the merits of the treatment on the basis of this case-study model. There are too many factors that might influence the measurement, and any judgment based on the One-Shot Case Study is tremendously suspect. For instance, the students may have performed just as well on the measurement if it were made prior to, rather than after, the treatment. Perhaps the treatment didn't affect the performance in any way, and the learners were essentially able to perform as well *before* the special homework exercises as after. The use of the One-Shot Case Study design makes it impossible to discover the impact of the treatment, which is what the teacher is really concerned about.

Another inadequate design that is sometimes used by teachers is called the *One-Group Pretest–Post-test Design*. This design is schematically depicted in Figure 2. In this instance the teacher administers a pretest measurement to his whole class, then administers the treatment (perhaps a newly devised lecture method involving carefully spaced rhetorical quostions), and then a post-treatment measurement. In other words, there

MEASUREMENT ▶ TREATMENT ▶ MEASUREMENT

Figure 2.   *One-Group Pretest–
Post-test Design*

is a measurement, then treatment, then measurement. This design also has serious weaknesses, because even if the teacher discovers that there is a sizable gain in pupil performance from pre- to post-test, there is the danger that it may be attributable to something other than the treatment. For instance, perhaps the learners *without* the treatment would have made the same pre- to post-test gains as a result of maturation or as a consequence of experiences completely removed from the school's control. The principal deficiency with the One-Group Pretest-Post-test design is that the teacher is unable to make strong inferences regarding the impact of the treatment.

The teacher can use a somewhat stronger but yet not thoroughly adequate design, the *Nonequivalent Control Group Design*. The Nonequivalent Control Group design is depicted in Figure 3, where an *M* is used to represent *Measurement* and a *T* to represent Treatment. The Nonequivalent Control

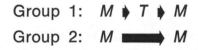

Group 1: *M* ♦ *T* ♦ *M*

Group 2: *M* ➡ *M*

Figure 3. *Nonequivalent Control Group Design*

Group Design involves a comparison of two groups that are selected "intact" for the research study. For instance, two classes might be compared with respect to their performance in an experimental situation. Two teachers, for example, might consider their classes sufficiently similar so that they attempt to see how well the students perform when one class receives a set of programed materials and the other does not. The design is an improvement over the previous two, and it is defensible to the extent that the groups tend to be equivalent. However, the design still has deficiencies in that it is extremely difficult to have "intact" groups that are really similar in important respects. There will be too many factors that elude the two teachers' attention but make the groups different. The danger with such comparisons is that any differential results may be primarily associated with the initial differences between the groups rather than with the impact of the treatment.

The question of equivalence of groups and the establishment of control groups raises an important point with respect to several procedures that might be used to establish group comparability. In the first place, you might think that you can employ "gain" scores—that is, post-instruction measurement minus pre-instruction measurement—such as when you administer the same test before and after instruction and subtract pretest from post-test scores. On the face of it, an average of these gain scores would appear to reflect the *relative* improvement of the two groups. But for a variety of reasons, gain scores have come into considerable disrepute among measurement specialists. To cite a very obvious deficiency in gain scores: it is far easier for a group with a *low* performance to make a large gain than it is for a group with a *high* pretest performance to do so. "Test ceiling" factors work against the gain potential of a group scoring very well on a pretest. It is much harder, for example, to move a class from the eightieth to the ninetieth percentiles on a standardized test than it is to move a class from the fortieth to the fiftieth percentiles. There are several other reasons why gain scores are not too serviceable, and, although we shall not elaborate these reasons here, you could certainly corroborate the generally negative feelings that researchers have regarding the use of gain scores by consulting any recent text in the field of educational measurement.

Another alternative that might occur to the teacher is to *match* the groups. Group matching has a time-honored tradition in the history of educational research, but in recent years the process of matching to equalize groups has been rejected as an unacceptable procedure by almost every prominent research-design expert. Although the reasons for this disapproval of matching are numerous, a simple explanation may suffice. For every variable on which groups are made equivalent via matching, there are probably twice as many relevant variables on which the groups are extremely different. These dissimilarities are very often more influential than the relatively few characteristics on which the groups are carefully matched. But the dissimilarities are often unidentified, and as a consequence groups may appear to be matched, whereas they are indeed very different with respect to variables that are strongly related to the dependent variable.

An efficient alternative to matching that is strongly recommended by research specialists is *randomization*. The use of randomization ensures initial equivalence of groups. If a teacher wishes to constitute two or more groups for an experimental contrast, he is urged to do so on the basis of a table of random numbers or by some other random procedure. He could, for example, put the names of all pupils on small pieces of paper, place them in a paper sack, and then randomly select them in such a way as to constitute his groups. If the teacher wished to form three equal groups for purposes of testing two experimental treatments along with an untreated control group, thirty names could be placed on small discs and then into a box. The first ten discs that the teacher selected would constitute Group A, the second ten Group B, and the remaining ten Group C. Once more, the teacher could turn to randomization in order to decide which group receives Treatment A, which group receives Treatment B, and which group serves as a control. The teacher could then place slips of paper with Group 1, Group 2, and Group 3 in the same box and decide that whichever group is initially selected will receive the first treatment, whichever group is selected second will receive the second treatment, and the remaining group will be the control group. A more efficient method of random assignment would be to use a table of random numbers. These tables are found in most statistics texts and are relatively easy to employ. By using random numbers tables a more refined randomization will result.

It might appear to you that randomization could result by chance in groups that are actually not equal. For example, with respect to obvious intelligence indices such as test scores, you might end up with randomly assigned groups that appear to be dissimilar. But, for every factor in which one group appears to be "more able," there are probably as many factors that have not been identified but that favor the "less able" group. Randomization, according to all established researchers, is the only respectable way to equalize groups. The teacher-experimenter is strongly advised to set up experimental groups in this fashion.

The possibilities of randomizing lead to a very powerful research design that the teacher can use to test the merits of a particular treatment. It is called the *Pretest-Post-test Control Group Design* and is depicted schematically in Figure 4. The

Group 1: *R M* ▶ *T* ▶ *M*
Group 1: *R M* ━━▶ *M*

Figure 4. *Pretest–Post test Control Group Design*

R in this model indicates that the two groups have been formed by randomization procedures prior to the initial measurement. The *M* and the *T* again refer to measurement and treatment. Since the initial equivalence of the two groups has been maximized through the use of randomization, this design allows the teacher to make strong inferences regarding the merits of a particular treatment.

A possible drawback of the Pretest-Post-test Control Group design is that certain types of pretreatment measures may have a confounding influence on the treatment. For example, the treatment *plus* the particular "learning set" established by the students' completion of the pretest may produce a post-test difference in favor of the treated group. Measurement procedures that, by their use, produce a change in the subject's behavior are known as *reactive* measures. If we administer an attitudinal questionnaire to learners prior to their viewing a film dealing with race relations, the completion of the questionnaire may unnaturally cue their reaction to the film. If the pretest measure appears to be reactive, an alternative to the Pretest-Post-test Control Group design should be employed.

The most likely alternative to the Pretest-Post-test Control Group design is the *Post-test Only Control Group Design*, which is represented in Figure 5. This design avoids the possible

$$\text{Group 1:} \quad R \ T \ \blacktriangleright \ M$$
$$\text{Group 2:} \quad R \qquad M$$

Figure 5. *Post-test Only Control Group Design*

contamination of reactive pretreatment measures. The comparison of the two groups' post-treatment measurements permits the teacher to make valid inferences regarding the value of the treatment. Even though teachers may be fearful of using this design because of their suspicions that randomly assigned groups will not be really equal, the randomization operation assures that comparisons made by this design are legitimate. The value of the design is that it eliminates the necessity of pretesting and, in the case of potentially reactive pretest measures, this consideration is very important.

Throughout this discussion we have been describing contrasts between two treatments. There may be many situations in which the teacher is anxious to compare the merits of three or more treatments. These can all be conducted through the use of the randomization procedures described earlier. Of course, the more students that are involved in any given treatment group, the more comfortable the teacher can be with respect to the results of the experiment. If, for instance, the teacher wished to test fifteen treatments and randomly divided a class of thirty students into groups of two students each, even though randomization procedures were used, one would be rather suspicious of the equivalence of the fifteen groups of only two pupils each.

The certainty that the teacher can place upon results gathered through such experiments depends upon the degree to which the teacher can control extraneous factors possibly influencing the post-instruction measurement. To the extent that these factors are controlled, the teacher can place considerable reliance on the results of his experiment. If he is unsure, he ought to replicate the study in another class (if he has one available) or perhaps during the next semester. A replication of a given study is always a strong way of confirming the legitimacy of the Inferences drawn from results of the initial experiment.

Sometimes the results of an experiment will be so dramatically in support of the predicted hypothesis that the teacher needs only to examine the data in very gross terms. For example, perhaps he only needs to compute a simple arithmetic mean of the two groups and can judge on the basis of a widespread superiority favoring one treatment that it, indeed, has been the more successful. On the other hand, if the performance of the groups has been almost identical, the teacher can readily conclude that there is no significant difference associated with the different treatments. In many situations, however, the results of the experiment will favor one group, but the teacher may be unsure whether the results really represent a significant phenomenon independent of chance. There are several statistics texts now available by which the teacher can quickly compute, often through statistical procedures that can be mastered within a relatively short period of time, the statistical significance of a given experimental result. By statistical significance the researcher means the statistical probability that the result of the experiment is a significant departure from what might be expected by chance alone.

Through the careful reading of the results of research conducted by others, together with the systematic conduct of small-scale experiments in his own classroom, the teacher can become a truly polished professional. Not only will he be using empirical methods to make better decisions regarding the modification of his instructional procedures, but he will also be constantly infusing his instructional arsenal with new evidence-supported treatments. Such treatments, since they are based on hard evidence rather than on capricious intuition, will undoubtedly lead to the improved attainment of instructional objectives.

ADDITIONAL READING

Campbell, Donald T., and Julian C. Stanley, *Experimental and Quasi-Experimental Designs for Research* (Chicago: Rand McNally & Company, 1967).

Hays, William L., *Statistics for Psychologists* (New York: Holt, Rinehart & Winston, Inc., 1963).

Popham, W. James, *Educational Statistics: Use and Interpretation* (New York: Harper & Row, Publishers, 1967).

Sax, Gilbert, *Empirical Foundations of Educational Research* (Englewood Cliffs, N.J.: Prentice-Hall, Inc., 1968).

Siegel, Sidney, *Nonparametric Statistics for the Behavioral Sciences* (New York: McGraw-Hill Book Company, 1956).

Index